THE
BEAUTIFUL GROUNDS 2

THE BEAUTIFUL GROUNDS 2

THROUGH THE NON-LEAGUE FOOTBALL CLUBS OF ENGLAND

RAY MARGETSON

ISBN 978-1-917558-03-7

001

Paperback Edition

© 2024 Margetson Publishing. All rights reserved.

No part of this publication may be reproduced, distributed, or transmitted in any form or by any means, including photocopying, recording, or other electronic or mechanical methods, without the prior written permission of the author/publisher, except in the case of brief quotations embodied in critical reviews and certain other non-commercial uses permitted by copyright law. For **permission requests, write to the author/ publisher**, addressed "Attention: Permissions Coordinator", at the address below:

raymargetson@btinternet.com

Designed & Formatted by UK Design Company, UK
Printed & Bound by CLOC Book Print, UK

Visit the Margetson Publishing website:

To my wife Eve (for her patience with this book!), and dedicated to my two children Christian and Hannah - for their belief in what I do.

CONTENTS

INTRODUCTION ix
AFC DUNSTABLE v WALTHAM ABBEY 10
AFC SUDBURY v STAMFORD 13
ALFRETON TOWN v WARRINGTON TOWN 16
ALNWICK TOWN v CHESTER LE STREET TOWN 18
AMERSHAM TOWN v ATHLETIC NEWHAM 21
ASCOT UNITED v GUERNSEY 23
ASHFORD TOWN (MIDDX) v HAMPTON & RICHMOND BOROUGH 26
AVELEY FC v HEMEL HEMPSTEAD 28
BADSHOT LEA v WINCHESTER CITY 31
BARKING TOWN v BRENTWOOD TOWN 34
BATH CITY v WELLING UNITED 37
BENFLEET v LITTLE OAKLEY 40
BERWICK RANGERS v BROOMHILL 43
BISHOP AUCKLAND v SHILDON 45
BISHOPS STORTFORD v SOUTHEND UNITED 48
BLYTH SPARTANS v KINGS LYNN TOWN 50
BOWERS & PITSEA v BRENTWOOD TOWN 53
BROOK HOUSE v BELSTONE 56
CAMBRIDGE CITY FC REVIEW 59
CHESHAM UNITED v BRAINTREE TOWN 62
CRAY WANDERERS v CRYSTAL PALACE 65
CROCKENHILL v FLEETDOWN UNITED RESERVES 68
CROOK TOWN v HOLKER OLD BOYS 70
CURZON ASHTON v BARNET 73
DIDCOT TOWN v OXFORD CITY 75
FARNHAM TOWN v JERSEY BULLS 78
GAINSBOROUGH TRINITY v WHITBY TOWN 81
GREAT YARMOUTH v WIVENHOE TOWN 84
HADLEY v AYLESBURY UNITED 87
HARBOROUGH TOWN v BURY 90
HENDON FC v WALTON & HERSHAM 93
HERNE BAY v NORTHWOOD 96

HERTFORD TOWN v HENDON TOWN	99
ILKESTON TOWN v BASFORD UNITED	102
KNAPHILL v AFC CROYDON ATHLETIC	105
LEAMINGTON v AFC SUDBURY	108
MICKLEOVER v AFC TELFORD UNITED	111
MILDENHALL TOWN v WROXHAM	114
NEWMARKET TOWN v WALTHAMSTOW	117
NORTH GREENFORD UNITED v ARDLEY UNITED	120
PETERBOROUGH SPORTS v DARLINGTON	122
RAMSGATE v CHICHESTER CITY	125
RAYNERS LANE REVIEW	128
ROMFORD v SPORTING BENGAL UNITED	131
RUSHALL OLYMPIC v BISHOPS STORTFORD	134
SAFFRON WALDEN TOWN v STANSTED	138
SCARBOROUGH ATHLETIC v ALFRETON TOWN	141
SELSEY v ROFFEY	145
SHEFFIELD FC v NANTWICH TOWN	148
SOLIHULL MOORS v WEALDSTONE	151
SOUTH SHIELDS v DARLINGTON	154
SOUTHEND UNITED v MAIDENHEAD UNITED	158
ST IVES TOWN v KETTERING TOWN	161
TADLEY CALLEVA v WOODLEY UNITED	164
TRING ATHLETIC v AYLESBURY VALE DYNAMOS	167
WARRINGTON RYLANDS v CHEADLE	170
WARRINGTON TOWN v SOUTHPORT	173
WELWYN GARDEN CITY v BIGGLESWADE TOWN	176
WHITBY TOWN v BASFORD UNITED	179
WINCHESTER CITY v MERTHYR TOWN	183
WORKSOP TOWN v SHEFFIELD WEDNESDAY	186
YATELEY UNITED v MOLESEY	189
BISHOP AUCKLAND MUSEUM	192
WOOLWICH WANDERERS v NEWTON HEATH	194
ACKNOWLEDGEMENTS	196

INTRODUCTION

Author, Ray Margetson, was born in Hackney, East London, in 1961.

Growing up playing football for both school and youth teams, he has also played non league football for Ilford FC, and secretary of that club.

Has coached youth teams for both Chichester City and Bosham, in West Sussex, whilst having FA coaching badges up to level 2 in the 2000's.

Earlier in the 1980's he was heavily involved in youth culture, with both fashion and music. Organising all day concerts, night clubs, as well as DJing, running a fanzine, alongside working in finance in the city. This was later followed by running a successful financial services company.

Has been well known for DJing live on various internet radio stations for around 9 years.

Has two grown up children - Christian & Hannah - who are both involved in music and acting respectively and both running their own businesses.

Married to wife Eve and living in London with mad English Springer Spaniel Charlie.

Author of the previous book - The Beautiful Grounds - a whistle stop humourous review of 180 different non league games in this country and Spain.

AFC DUNSTABLE V WALTHAM ABBEY
SOUTHERN LEAGUE DIVISION 1 CENTRAL PLAY OFF SEMI FINAL

01/05/24

Tonight's play off semi final is over to Bedfordshire for AFC Dunstable v Waltham Abbey.

In speaking with new Chairmen Dan Bedi, the club is made up of a really youthful home side of players between 16-22, and an average age of 19....nnnnnnn nineteen! The club, and team, has dramatically changed within a season. With a very low budget they are attracting high quality youth players, and ex professionals from higher divisions. How? Because of what the club can offer under the overall company of 'Varsity 9', who have successfully taken over the club, offering excellent coaching, conditioning, analysts, and potential college scholarships in the USA and a possible route into the MLS.

Varsity 9 were born out of 'Soccer assist' and have joint managers James Oxley & James Townsend at the helm. The club groundshare with Dunstable Town and rent the pitch on match day & training from Central Bedfordshire council who own the ground, and Bedfordshire FA who run the facilities. The club are looking to stay at this ground - Creasy Park - until they reach the football league! AFC generate their own income through gate receipts and sponsors where incidentally the crowds have gone up from 120/150 to 250, and tonight's attendance is well over 500. The club plans to open a new academy at the ground and to extend the entire facilities in the near future, including 2 x new 4g pitches behind the end goal. The whole ethos at the club is 'progression'

and becoming very sustainable. Varsity 9 are looking at elite young players going through their academy, to play a year in the UK then go off to the USA for a scholarship. They are able to recruit better players as they also build relationships with other clubs for loan players. They've currently had young players from Fulham, Chelsea, Luton, and Hitchin. The bond between all these young players is great and they receive excellent coaching backed up by top physios, strength & conditioning coaches, and analysts, which improve their playing and fitness levels all round. This is a totally different and unique way of running a football club and a club to look out for in the future. Considering they have one of the lowest budgets in the league their culture is harmonious with no star players. This is a fantastic pathway for players to progress through the leagues and will no doubt have scouts watching their games every week. They currently have 26 youth teams affiliated to the club and their coaches run youth academies at Luton FC. Their ladies team is currently very successful and it's the local community they really tap into. They give back through football - working with lots of children and their families who are underprivileged and all U12's get free entry at games.

So far, during the goalless first half of this game, the standard of football is pretty good, and evenly matched ,between two very good footballing sides, and then on the stroke of HT Waltham Abbey go in front from a neat move and a good side foot into the net. Dunstable are back in the frame with an early second half equaliser. The home team are in the ascendency now as they go into the lead 2-1. Then an overhead kick from Waltham Abbey, which was going in for the equaliser until the keeper made a great diving save to catch the ball. It's the AFC fans making all the noise now, and it's not just from their vuvuzelas!.... then at the death after 6 added mins it's the equaliser!...and so to extra time and

suddenly a great hush around the ground. Half way through the first half it's now 3-2 to the Abbey. A minute later and it's a penalty to AFC...now it's 3-3! The crowd behind the embankment goal are going crazy and the noise levels crank up. At the other end the Abbey let fly with a shot which the keeper fingertips over the bar. What next?! 3-3 after extra time and on to penalties. Now 4-4 after 5 pens each....Finally after 20 pens in total it's 8-7 to Waltham Abbey. Probably the match of the season with a crowd of over 525 here.

The previous chairman and footballing legend here - Simon Bullard - put the club up for sale last year for a £1. Simon was at the helm for 29 years as chairman/president/player. They had 12 bidders but Varsity 9 seemed the best way forward for the club and here you can see the results of the success over the past year. It's nice to see the club have kept the original badge when the club first started out as Old Dunstablians. This was the grammar school which was formed in 1981 and was renamed AFC Dunstable in 2004. The club moved to their current ground in 2008 as the lower of the clubs ground sharing here. Now the club are the higher placed team over Dunstable Town and take precedence over the fixtures played here. They only pay £135 per game inc food for match days. The council pay all the other outgoings including the floodlights, so a very good deal here. The club has come a long way since starting in the Dunstable Alliance Football League in 1983.

They achieved status as **an FA Charter Standard Community club in 2008**. The furthest they have gone in the **FA cup was in the** 3rd qualifying round v Peterborough Sports. I expect this will be improved upon very soon. Aside from the badge, they've kept their nick**name as** the OD**'s** (Old Dunst**ab**lians**)**.

The whole ethos is about Progression and they are very sustainable. They have a committee of 8-10 plus a legal board as well....and they play great attractive football.

AFC SUDBURY V STAMFORD
SOUTHERN LEAGUE CENTRAL PREMIER DIVISION
14/09/24

Over to sunny Suffolk in todays glorious sun, in the south of the county, to see AFC Sudbury v Stamford. 8th v 1st in this Southern League Premier Central Division.

The contrast in playing styles are that the home team have more of an attacking free flow style, whereas the away team are tighter in defence and good at set pieces. Speaking with Chairman Andrew Long - who took over as chairman in 2018, after joining the club the year before. He originally came along via playing golf with the former chairman to help the club out with issues. He is actually a former player himself with Stourbridge, and Halesowen as originally from the Midlands.

I'm informed of the merger, back in 1999 between two local clubs namely Sudbury Town & Sudbury Wanderers. The A in AFC, by the way, stands for amalgamated. Both clubs were in financial difficulty, so it made sense to merge, or at least to outsiders it did! The proceeds from the sale of the Town ground was used to finance the restructuring of the current ground, where the Wanderers used to play on. The Town played in yellow and the Wanderers in blue, so a happy medium was made with AFC Sudbury playing in both yellow and blue. The 3G pitch was built 8 1/2 years ago and is still looking good, with the clubhouse built back in 2001 and still looking fairly new!

The club own their ground and stadium outright including a piece of land at the far end - which could be used for developing in the future. It currently has a restricted covenant on for sport only but could potentially be lifted for the

future. The logical conclusion would be to provide a full time school here with football content i.e. sports science, as with the clubs academy they promote the school first(education)and football second. There is also a gym nearby to that land, that is being rented to the club for use by the academy & first team, as well as a room for physio treatment.

This club, I might add, is 100% fan owned. Entirely run by the supporters, and all officials are unpaid volunteers. They currently have 37 teams all told and are renowned as a family club. This includes a thriving academy for both boys and girls, of which both teams are currently National college champions. There is most definitely a pathway from youth to first team with ex players such as Josh Stokes going to Bristol City and Liam Bennett going to Cambridge United. Liam incidentally, has never forgotten his roots and comes back to the club and coaches here voluntarily.

The club want to make this the largest community leisure centre in South Suffolk/North Essex - to provide a safe location to play and watch sport. Unusually they have a memorial gardens, situated next to the Union Jack flag with yellow Suffolk on it! The club have received a grant from Sport England/Football Foundation to build another 3G pitch at the front to the ground, which is currently used as a grass pitch for training facilities. In effect football clubs are now taking over from local authorities to supply training facilities for the youth of the area. This is a substantial community involvement as the current demand is so great with their

existing 3G pitch. The club see this as their responsibility to provide facilities 7 days a week up to 10pm at night. The original, and current, 3G pitch was financed by the club and shareholders. The volunteers, like Ben(the organiser of volunteers) are the lifeblood of the club and above the entrance to the turnstiles is dedicated in memory to Lynsey(Ben's wife)who recently died of cancer and was described as 'a real force of nature'.

When the club were in the Isthmian League, they were voted in the top 2 for fans visiting their ground, and top of the respect league for advocating no bad language here for everyone from player's, fans, officials, and respect for all. The club work well with the local community and had zoom meetings with the fans, during covid, to keep the contact going. The link with charities is to do with health and well being, both mental and physical. At every home fans they have a designated charity to support. The chairman quotes "I believe in what the club is trying to do. If it's just about glory for the club then I wouldn't be interested!"

As for todays game it was a 3-0 home victory, which could have been more as Sudbury missed a penalty and also hit the post. Attendance of 377.

ALFRETON TOWN V WARRINGTON TOWN
NATIONAL LEAGUE NORTH

07/10/23

Over to Al'ton in Derbyshire this afternoon, via the A2/A12/M11/M25/M1/A38. National League North - Alfreton Town v Warrington Town.

One of the most friendliest and welcoming clubs I've come across, if not thee friendliest.

A history going back to the merger of 2 clubs - Alfreton Miners Welfare and Alfreton United - back in 1959....oh, hold up its 1-0 to Alfreton after 17 mins!....ground built back then and supported by the local authority. Most of the ground is fitted with seats. Behind one goal the red seats were donated from Kettering Towns old ground. The blue seats, opposite the players tunnel, were donated from Leicester City's old ground, and the turnstiles from Maine Road, Man.City's old ground.

Mend and make do lad!

Lovely meeting up with secretary **Andrew** Raisin, Chairman Wayne Bradley, Stadium announcer and unofficial historian Bill Draper who's been here since man & boy - forever!...and Billy Heath the Manager, who I last saw at the Tamworth game, who made a great little reply to the Tamworth supporters who were berating him through the game!

We go into the second half now 1-1 after Warrington equalise just before HT.....and it stays that way till the end.

Alfreton need to up their game against Macclesfield in the cup next week.

The record attendance at North street is

5,023 v Matlock Town in 1960. Then in 1997 Wayne Bradley took over as Chairman with the club in the Northern Counties League. A few years later in 2001/02, the club achieved unprecedented success with Chris Wilder as manager and landed four trophies - Northern Counties(East)League Premier Division, League cup, Presidents cup, and the Derbyshire Senior cup. Promotion back to the Northern Premier League was followed by entering into the Conference north.

The club today operates a Football in the Community coaching scheme in partnership with the National League Trust, with around 1600 children receiving fully qualified tuition each year from the full time coaching staff, in addition to hosting numerous community groups.

2007/08 saw new boss Nicky Laws take over. The following season the club finished in their highest ever position of 3rd in Conference north, narrowly losing out in the semi final play offs to AFC Telford United, and also reaching the 2nd round of the FA cup. Then in 2009/20 they again finished 3rd and went on to lose in the final of the play offs this time to Fleetwood Town. Third time lucky as the next season they won that division by a clear 10 points. This culminated in their highest ever position playing at step 1 level. Now back in the National League North amd aiming to push on again.

ALNWICK TOWN V CHESTER LE STREET TOWN
NORTHERN LEAGUE DIVISION 2

13/08/24

Second game in a week in Northumberland and a competitive English game at step 6 level in the Northern League Division 2 - Alnwick Town v Chester Le Street Town.

This is the most northerly English club playing at this level and above in England. Alnwick play at the original St James Park, not like the copycats over at Newcastle United and a fantastically friendly little club with a big(lion)heart. Talking about lions as they have been allowed to have the rampart lion on their club shirts which is part of the heraldic symbol used by the Duke of Northumberland as he has given the club permission to use it! The Duchess has given her 'Fleur de ly' emblem for the juniors club to wear as a badge on their shirts.

Current chairman, Tommy McKie, has been at the helm now for 17 years and took over when the club were only 2 weeks from 'going to the wall'. Bulldozers were at the ready until Tommy went along to Alnwick Castle, met the Duke of

Northumberland himself, and amazingly came away, after asking for £100K to save the club, with an offer of £20Kp.a. over the next 5 years. Job done and was also promised as much land as you need to improve the club and move on. A great transformation, as reported back in 2010, of the club and now having 32 teams at the club(28 of those at youth level). The Duke came to watch the Juniors, with 100 kids turning up on that occasion. The club needed 2 teams to start with and with his help have developed into 28 teams. They also have the field and land for junior facilities, all owned by the Duke, but for use of the club. The club now have enough land for facilities and to gradually develop on for the future.

The club were originally founded in 1893 but more than likely go even further back to 1879. The research requested by the Duke shows the club potentially played on this ground back in 1893, and there is a codicile in place that football be played on this ground only.

The scoreline tonight stands at 0-0 at HT and Alnwick, playing their 6th league game of the season have drawn 2, lost 2, and won 1 so far. The game was eventually won 1-0 by the away team, and a learning curve in this division.

For any future promotion to division 1, in this league, they would need to install 100 seats together. The average crowd mid week is around 130, increasing to 200 on Saturdays. This is a lot of peoples second team around these parts. The manager, Richie, has a great sway in getting players up here to the club, which obviously helps from where they are positioned geographically. A big shout to their main sponsor Thornburn who are very supportive financially to the club.

Any expansion plans for the future, the Duke is fully behind the club. The 25 year lease on the ground, the club have an option to renew. However, they can't say no due to the covenant! The future looks great for Alnwick Town FC, thanks largely due to Tom McKie's meeting with the Duke of Northumberland, and the Duke's kind offer of all the facilities, land, and financial support to kick start the club going forward.

Little did you know that the club were voted recently the 7th best ground in the Northern League…..and the Duke of Northumberland is the clubs President!…. do check out this club on your travels around the castles of this beautiful county of Northumberland, the county of castles.

AMERSHAM TOWN V ATHLETIC NEWHAM
FA CUP 1ST QUALIFYING ROUND
03/09/24

Off to the second most westerly line on the London Metropolitan Underground, for tonight's replay of this FA cup 1st qualifying round.

It's Amersham Town v Athletic Newham in this countryside setting. Buckinghamshire v East London. Hoping for some goals after the first game ended at 3-3 on Saturday.

It was a 23 minute walk from the station, through literally countryside and across railway tracks to get there!

The club was founded in 1890 but from the look of some old photos in the clubhouse, the ground hasn't changed much since the 1920's. There is one old main stand with a scattering of loose seats at the back. Opposite this stand are the dug outs and a walkway and likewise behind one goal. Behind the other goal is just sectioned off. The changing rooms are in a separate room away from the clubhouse and with a few steps up to the pitch. The ground has been levelled over recent years, as it was on a 11 foot steep slope from the main stand going downwards, and they've extended the clubhouse bar/kitchen. No programme - online was the answer - and no turnstiles. It's just two guys sitting at a fold up table collecting as fans come along!

Both teams are at step 5 level - Amersham are in the Combined Counties League Premier Division North, after being promoted from step 6 last season, winning the title with 111 goals scored, and Newham in the Essex Senior League. Burgess Hill Town await the winners in the next round....which Amersham win with a resilient 1-0 victory in front of a larger than usual crowd of 149.

What actually has changed at the club is in 2006, the old shelving in the dressing rooms has gone - this was originally prepared during the war as it was used as a mortuary, for laying the expected dead bodies on during the war! The pitch was also levelled at that time, and youth pitches were built across the road. This was land that was leased from the Tyrwitt- Drake family, descendants from the famous Sir Francis Drake. They have also extended the clubhouse and added new floodlights, of which the club raised 30% and the rest from the Football Foundation. They are situated in an area of outstanding natural beauty, therefore it's very difficult to improve, and seating would be a problem as they need a new stand with additional seating.

ASCOT UNITED V GUERNSEY
ISTHMIAN LEAGUE SOUTH CENTRAL
26/08/23

Over to Ascot today, no it's not horse racing for a change but instead to see the mighty Ascot United take on the French team - Guernsey FC!

So, an England v France international....or is it Berkshire v Channel Islands?!

Ascot have won their league last season and are now promoted to this Isthmian South Central Division. Not withstanding that they won the FA Vase at Wembley so a double winning season. Half an hour into the game and Ascot are 1-0 up so continuing with their winning momentum.

Spoke with the Chairman - Simon Negus - and Secretary Ricky who are filling me in with the recent history of the club. Great meeting the director of Guernsey - Nigel Braybrook - who lives only a short walk from me. Small world! Looks like Guernsey are missing their top striker Ross Allen who for some reason can't make it today

Anyway, what a great little ground here at Ascot. Definitely a club on the up - watch out Man City they'll be chasing you soon!

A great clubhouse/bar, new 3G pitch - well 4 years old but still looks great. Modern dug outs and all very much akin to Tuesdays game at Cobham FC. Nicely designed and compact hospitality suite situated near one of the corner flags. A seated area as a main grandstand and plenty of standing room outside the clubhouse - very much needed when the rain, and lightning, came down.

Ascot go in 2-0 at half time.....and not too long into the second half get a third coolly slotted home by no.10. Now it's 4-0 with a last minute goal....with 4 mins added time. Attendance of 189.

Ascot United FC claims to be the biggest grassroots football club in the country. They certainly have the facilities that are the envy of many other clubs, but are happy to share these facilities with other parts of the community where they can. The Foundation academy is the youngest playing section for boys and girls age 4 and 5, having around 100 kids signed up for weekly sessions. They also provide a girls development centre with 40-50 girls each week.

The Junior section is the heartbeat of the club with 63 boys teams and 10 girls teams playing in a variety of leagues on over the weekend. At some age groups there could be up to 9 different squads playing!

As the Juniors progress, there is a pathway to senior football. Each year sees some of their players depart to professional clubs and academy set ups. However, the JPL and Allied U18 squads give a chance for the youngsters to make it to the first team. They also have their Warrior squad who are affiliated with the Special Olympics GB providing resources to get them to play against other mixed ability teams across the country. A thriving vets section have two teams playing in the West London vets league with some of the 'oldies' helping out at the club as well as with the Junior teams. The women's adult teams are successful of recent seasons winning cups and league and it seems the club as a whole are flourishing.

The first record of Ascot United was chronicled in 1928 with teams of that name forming and re forming until 1965 and playing at Sunninghill. From 1990 the club really started to take shape when a new clubhouse was erected at the Racecourse Ground. A new 11 a side pitch and training area were constructed on what is now the 3G and top mini pitch. 2004 - the club were awarded FA Charter Community club status. 2006 - Success winning the Reading Senior League and promotion to the Hellenic League 1st Division East. 2010 - with the help of the Football Foundation, a new clubhouse and other facilities were built, runners up in their league, and promoted to the Hellenic Premier League.

2011- First appearance in the FA cup and the first game to be screened live by Facebook, with a ground crowd record of 1,150. Going on to 2022, another new record attendance of 1,267 when they defeated Wycombe Wanderers in the Berks & Bucks Senior cup.

2022/23 - Champions of the Combined Counties League Premier Division North with 102 points and promotion for the first time to step 4, allied with winning the FA Vase cup for a League and cup double.

The Yellas have come an awful long way in a short space of time since their promotion from step 7 in 2007.

Get along to one of their games soon and also view the Ascot racecourse from one of the corner flags at the same time!

ASHFORD TOWN (MIDDX) V HAMPTON & RICHMOND BOROUGH

PRE SEASON FRIENDLY

15/07/23

Game 1 of our double header today takes us over to Middlesex, even though the roads have Surrey County Council signs up on the way to the ground!

Anyway it's Heathrow Airport area, with the planes flying nearby. Leaving Hatton Cross tube to get the 203 bus, then a walk down Long Lane/Short Road and arrived!

A pre season friendly between Ashford United(Middx), who survived the drop from the Isthmian South Central Division last season, and Hampton & Richmond who are placed two divisions higher in the National South League.

Ashford in their orange & white tops, and Hampton in their away tops sporting the blue and white Argentina look!

The ground consists of seated areas alongside the length of the pitch, and one small covered behind one goal, and the other goal area an open walk way with heavy industrial style barbed wire and fencing backing onto what looks like an oil refinery.

To the game - early on Hampton had a fantastic chance one on one with the Ashford keeper, but

failed in an attempt to score as he shot straight at the keepers legs(easier to go round the keeper in my opinion). Within a minute Hampton are 1-0 up. 36 minutes gone and it's 2-0 to the visitors.

During the interval I met up and had a beer with the Ashford Chairman Nick.

You seriously won't meet a more lovelier, friendly and welcoming guy at a club than him.

A windy start to the second half, even in the bright sunshine, and more of the same with Hampton attacking. However, a few subs later for Ashford and they get a goal back. Some good work from sub no.19 gets finished off by sub no.11. Then we have another 5 subs on for Ashford, after the initial three.

Final score of 2-1 to Hampton and what looks like a seriously injured sub for Ashford right at the end.

Originally founded in 1958, Ashford were founder members of the Surrey Premier League back in 1982. In 1989 they were runners up and won the Surrey premier cup. The club are both affiliated to the Middlesex FA and the Surrey FA.

Their current ground in Short Lane, Stanwell, has been host to the club since 1986, and has a capacity of 2,550, of which 250 is seated and covered. The ground was renamed the Robert Parker stadium in 2010 in honour of Bob Parker who had served as Chairman for 28 years.

AVELEY FC V HEMEL HEMPSTEAD
NATIONAL LEAGUE SOUTH

06/11/23

Across the Dartford tunnel and over to good old Esssseeexxx...to see Aveley at home to Hemel Hempstead. Aveley currently second to Yeovil in this division, and deservedly so with some great attacking football. Two promotions on the trot for Aveley and potentially a third! How have they achieved this? Well I caught up with the Secretary, and CEO, Craig Johnson to find out more

The teams come out to Blurs 'Parklife'. Aveley resplendent in all blue(with a bit of white!)and Hemel in their away kit of all green with white sleeves.

Half time and all square at 0-0 despite lots of attacking, and we're treated to more Blur with 'Song 2'. Hmmm almost expect Damon Albarn to come out on the pitch soon!...

To the start of Aveley - formed in 1927 and moved to Millfield in 1952.

Prior to their move to Parkside, there was a 7 year plan to develop. They found out the developers could build on their brown belt land, and a new sports hub was in the offing at Belhus Park. March

2014 - the plan to develop started and in August 2017 their new ground was built. All the while though the club smartly carried on playing at their old ground, so a smooth transition, unlike other clubs who have sold their ground to developers, moved out, and eventually gone out of existence. Their previous ground was 500 yards up the road where all the new houses are built on.

Craig started off in the youth team, graduated to the 1st team, left then came back as player/manager. He was 4 1/2 years as manager before finally becoming club secretary and also CEO.

Their current promotion means they have until March 2024 to come up with £250K to complete ground grading requirements. They should get 50/65% from the football foundation but need to find the rest themselves. If they don't, they get relegated no matter where they finish in the league. Those are the rules! However, it gets done of course.

They are very much a community based club and are currently within this division punching above their weight. They have 22 youth teams, Academy, vets, and ladies teams.

To quote "we will take promotion and see what happens!"...

...on 61 mins Aveley take the lead from a corner. 62 mins it's now 2-0 with a header from Harry Gibbs via a free kick. 87 mins the ref blows for a penalty to Hemel after a trip in the box. Now 2-1, and a nervy end, as Hemel nearly score in the 95th minute but the header goes straight into the keepers arms. Sighs all round as it's finishes a 2-1 home win. Despite Aveley selling two of their top players to Solihull Moors, and competitors in this division - Maidstone United - they are now currently joint top of this division with Yeovil.

A fantastic achievement.

BADSHOT LEA V WINCHESTER CITY
PRE SEASON FRIENDLY
04/07/23

HALLELUJAH!! It's the first game of the season - albeit a pre season friendly of course. So, we find ourselves in darkest Surrey, on the way to Hampshire, and a first time visit to Badshot Lea.

Tonight they play host to Winchester City of the Southern League Premier Division. Badshot were runners up to champions Raynes Park Vale(from SW London)last season and now find themselves promoted to step 4, and the Isthmian South Central Division. A hailstorm, of biblical proportions, hasn't stopped this game going ahead. Yes, the pitch needed it but will make it a lot softer now to play on.

Average attendance seemed to be appx 150 last season, although they did manage crowds of well over 300 in 3 of their games.

Going in at half time, Winchester are 1-0 up, and seem the more self assured and their passing is a lot quicker. Badshot are still in the game though and not making it easy for their opponents at a higher level. Then the second half.... Winchester score three quick goals in six minutes and the game looks over. 0-4 to the away team and we've only just got going in the second half!.....now 5-0 to the City!....near the end Badshot don't give up and hit the post, only for Winchester a minute later to score their 6th. So a final score line of 0-6. A big difference it seems and a great test to start the new season for Badshot.

BADSHOT LEA FOOTBALL CLUB

WELCOME TO THE OPERATIX COMMUNITY GROUND
HOME OF BADSHOT LEA FOOTBALL CLUB

SALES ACCELERATION
OPERATIX ∞

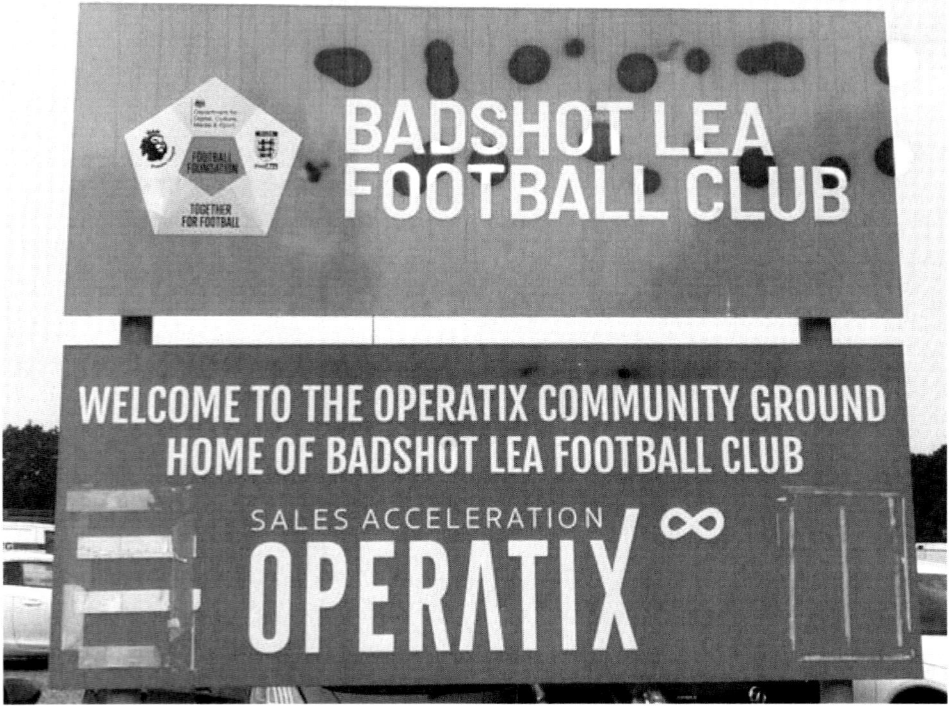

The club were originally formed in 1904 - although they only played friendly matches until joining the Surrey County FA in 1907. In the 1930's they won the Surrey Intermediate League two years on the trot. In 1985/86 they won the division again being promoted to the Surrey Premier League. After promotions, relegations, and restructuring of the leagues, they arrived in the Combined Counties League in 2007. That was the year the club left the old Recreation ground as it failed ground grading, and ground shared at Farnborough, Godalming Town, Ash United, Camberley Town, developed the former Farnham rugby club ground in Wrecclesham , before finally moving into their current ground in Westfield Lane in 2019.

Now enjoying life in the Isthmian League South Central Divsion.

BARKING TOWN V BRENTWOOD TOWN
PRE SEASON FRIENDLY

19/07/24

Pre season Essex derby friendly tonight - Barking v Brentwood Town - the all whites of Barking at step 5 of the Essex Senior League, v Step 4 Brentwood in all orange of the Isthmian North Division.

Getting the run down on Barking through project manager, Mark Harris, who informs me that their 3G pitch, development in 2020, is used 7 days a week. Built by Velocity and been passed again this year by FIFA for "Pro Quality" standard. Expansion plans include a new clubhouse to be built behind the metal stand which is proposed to be relocated behind the technical area.

The New Community Clubhouse will be a multi function usage as the 1st floor will be made into classrooms with sliding walls to open up to a large function room for events.

The opposite end of the ground to the clubhouse there is a proposal to install an additional 3G Astro pitch. This requirement is due to the growth of both the local community and the clubs ever growing number of teams to around 30.

Romford FC are ground sharing this year after they suddenly moved away from the old East Thurrock ground they moved into. Ilford FC will be moving back to their own Cricklefields ground.

Barking's previous ground was at Vicarage Fields, in the centre of town, which they lost back in 1973, after the local council moved them to build a new road - which didn't happen!

Rob O'Brien, the Chairman, tells me that the late 70's were the most successful time in Barking's history, even beating Oxford United back in '79.

They had Eddie McCluskey who managed them from 1970-80 and who went onto further success at Enfield FC.

The ground itself - the main seated stand runs practically the length of one side of the pitch. It was partly the original stand of '73 and has been extended since to 250 seats and a proposal to extend further to a row of 4 row stands(which gets up to step 3 standard).

The bar, from the club house, looks out onto the pitch, is carpeted in astro turf on the outside, and covered shielding it from the elements.

The club is a non for profit club, is self financing with various members running the club.

They have a Jack Leslie campaign on - Leslie being a prolific scorer at Plymouth but sold by Barking to them for a single £10 note, back in the 1920's. He was the first black player listed to play for England. When the FA saw he was black,

he wasn't picked to play for his country. The FA eventually awarded a posthumous cap many years after his death. Barking FC are proud to have helped Jack Leslie further his footballing career in the professional game. The club have helped many players go pro and have great professional careers.

After Jacks playing days, he used to clean the boots at West Ham under John Lyall until he retired in 1982. The club supported the statue erected at Plymouth Argle FC in his honour and what he stood for. A stone at the foot of the Statue states this is supported by Barking FC.

Recent players that have gone on to a higher level are - Kennedy Dariri(was on a contract)and sold to Grays Athletic at step 4. Isaac Westendorf sold to Newcastle United for £10K, who then went on loan to Larne and won the Northern Ireland championship, also playing in the Champions League for them(Larne that is not Newcastle!)

Barking have a positive relationship with the local council, and were the first club/organisation to work with the council when they bought into their healthy lifestyle campaign with the council.

They now have 30 teams including youth, girls, ladies, vets, Sunday team, scholarship, and an open policy for SEN with fun games - engagement in the local community.

They have improved the club from top to bottom to enable it to support the community in many ways. The new Community Clubhouse is needed more than ever for them to continue this supportive journey.

BATH CITY V WELLING UNITED
NATIONAL LEAGUE SOUTH

23/12/23

This years pre Christmas festive game takes us to the Roman city of Bath - hosting this National League South fixture v Welling. Bath - the Romans - are doing quite well this season. Welling not so.

The ground is even more unique, than say Altrincham, as a real charming old fashioned non league ground. Even the covered terracing, opposite the main stand has a sloping sideways terrace! Both terraces behind the goals are open. The main stand also houses underneath, the dressing rooms, bar, boardroom, and adjacent to it a smaller stand alone stand.

First goal, and blood, to the Romans in the 23rd min through Scott Wilson. Coming up to HT and the young starlet of the team - Jordan Thomas - puts away the second from a great cross.

Into the second half and Bath now 3-0 up, through Dan Hayfield, in the 56th min, with a deft flicked header across goal into the far corner of the net. Sublime.

Still time for a 4th in the 87th min. A penalty assuredly put away by Cody Cooke after a trip in the box.

Man of the match is Jordan Thomas and attendance, a lower than average 1,103 after having to compete with Bath rugby playing against Harlequins and Christmas shoppers.

The club itself is a supporters own club with 53% of the shares. The rest are owned by individuals. The structure has changed considerably since Bristol

Rovers left as tenants. In fact it changed in 2000 in favour of the supporters. The club raised funds to buy shares and three of the directors retained the shares. As a group of individuals they got up to 25% to stop anyone selling the ground and thereby continuing with the club as security for the future. There are in actual fact only four people employed at the club(besides the players of course)and the rest of 'staff' are all volunteers.

In speaking with football chairman, Paul Williams, there is potential development at the club. A planning application submitted in 2020 was for new stands, 3G pitch, student accommodation building blocks. This was denied by the council. However the 3G pitch has been accepted and will be going ahead, and there will be plans for refurbishing the ground as opposed to completely developing.

The average attendance has increased from 1,100 last season to 1500/1600 this season. This has been boosted by the community day that the club has held. It's also one of the rare grounds where the bar is outside the ground!

John Reynolds, a director, who joined the board in 2004, is a major shareholder and the club has been a part of his life since age 6, and is now, at age 77, one of the most friendliest characters you could ever meet.

Going back to the 1950's they would get 18,500 for a cup tie with Bolton. Back in the days when life for a working class kid would be football and boxing, and that's it!

I've been regaled of tales of air raid shelters behind both goals(sadly no longer there!) The original ground reached right down to the High Street.

Their most famous players are namely Malcolm Allison and Tony Book. Malcolm spent time at West Ham before becoming famous with his fedora and cup runs at Palace. Malcolm took Tony Book down to Plymouth, then Tony moved onto Man City where he captained their FA cup winning side.

The club have produced good players in the past, with good development coming through their system to the present day.

Great meeting up with East End Hammer Tim Mardell who we travelled to watch England in the 1986 World Cup in Mexico. Was even introduced to top manager Jerry Gill today.

This is easily one of my overall top 10 non league clubs. Go and visit before the ground gets completely refurbished!

BENFLEET V LITTLE OAKLEY
ESSEX SENIOR LEAGUE

17/09/24

Over to Essex tonight for the step 5 clash between Benfleet and Little Oakley. Benfleet, newly promoted to the Essex Senior League for the first time in their history, having previously been in the Eastern Counties Division 1 South. As it stands it's 5th v 10th in this division.

We're only 6 weeks into the club playing at their newly revamped ground. In speaking with Chairman, Dan Wright, he's been 'blown away by the support from the local community, fans and sponsors alike'. The crowds are definitely turning up with an average 200 now. Over £20K has recently come in from sponsors with £5K pa alone coming in from a local company - Utility Safety Solutions. Tonight it could be Benfleet v Benfleet, as Oakley have turned up with the same kit as the home side and are playing in Benfleets away kit! I hope they pay the laundry bill tonight! Kick off has been delayed 14 mins due to this.

The club has a real community feel about it, after speaking with secretary Gary, and is rightly enthusiastic about how the club is progressing. A new pitch, new seated stand and 2 x covered terraces. New surrounds enclosing the pitch and walkways. The clubhouse is ongoing being refurbed with new heating about to go in, a revamped games room to the rear of the bar, and there are two trophy cabinets noticeably displayed packed with silverware, which would put many other clubs to shame!

The dream for the club is for step 3/4 level and getting crowds up to 1,000 for big games. Regards expansion plans, the club are getting surveyors in, in preparation for potential promotion to steps 4 & 3, so that they will be ahead of the game in that respect. Currently they are looking at getting another 150 seat stand, 2 small terraced stands behind both goals, and it's just as well the local council are very supportive in their plans. They even turn up for the games!

Although the land is owned by the local council, it is on a 35 year lease and potentially they could utilise all surrounding green area, where their training and youth pitches are, and make use of them. The investors are local businessman including Keith Wells, who has the current main stand named after his father. He regularly uses his connections to help the club. The youth teams are all based locally and likewise with the sponsors, making it a real big community family feel to the club.

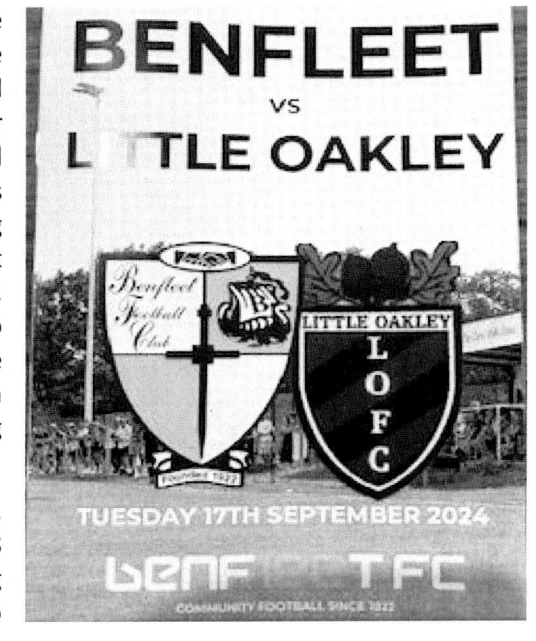

There are currently 20 teams, playing behind the stadium, and 8 pitches, but they are now having to turn teams away! They are, to quote, "well looked after" and it's best to have teams to actually engage with, rather than have quantity.

The history of the club goes back 102 years to when the club was formed in 1922. In 1972 winning the Southend & District league, then getting promoted to the Essex Olympian League. 1989 becoming champions of the Essex Intermediate League & also the cup in their double winning season....until last seasons record breaking league title winning season with 103 points....oh, and they have Cameron Harris at centre back, son of former Millwall player and manager Neil Harris. 14 mins into the game and it's 0-1 followed by the equaliser 2 mins later. In a fairly even game it's Benfleet who get the winner in the 2nd half and hold on for the 3 points with a 2-1 win. An Essex club definitely going places.

BERWICK RANGERS V BROOMHILL
SCOTTISH LOWLAND LEAGUE

10/08/24

Onto Scottish lowland (non) league with a difference. Here at Shielfield Park, the home to Berwick Rangers, the only English club to play competitive football in the Scottish League. Today they host Broomhill and Berwick already have 9 points, having won their first 3 games. If they win today then the last time they won 4 games on the trot was when they won the Scottish League Division two!

Greeted at the main entrance by stadium director Robert Johnson, who gave us a guided tour of the stadium and welcoming Charlie our English Springer Spaniel. The club, although founded in 1871, came here in 1953. They previously played on the old pitch behind the old covered terrace known as the 'ducket' stand. Ducket is another name for pigeons loft so you can see who lives there! The ground is really impressive and that's not just the two stands but the wide expanse of the whole stadium. Yes, it hosts a speedway track which is regularly used every Saturday night and generates great income for the club. A very unique ground and if you've not been, then it's a must for every football fan to go to, and believe me I've been to a number already!

The main stand, with updated floodlights, is a nicely covered main seated stand covering the length of the pitch. Behind both goals are all open, and the old stand opposite is akin to the old stands at Workington AFC. That old stand originally came from the old Bradford Park Avenue ground. There are plenty of barriers all around the perimeters of the pitch, basically as safety for the speedway riders crashing into the crowds and vice Versa!

The clubs most famous victory must be in 1967, beating Glasgow Rangers 1-0 in the Scottish Cup 1st round, in front of a crowd of 13,365. Sammy Reid scoring the winner. The crowds are a healthy 515 now (which was the attendance at the last home game). The club are generating higher attendances now compared to when they were higher up in the Scottish Division 2 when they were more like 250. The new Chairman, Kevin Dixon, who took over the club In February 2023, has gradually upgraded a number of the facilities here. Not only that but brought the community a lot closer together. Before he joined, the club had been neglected and he's soon over seen upgrading the facilities.

BISHOP AUCKLAND V SHILDON
NORTHERN LEAGUE DIVISION 1
01/04/24

Third game in four days, over Easter, in County Durham....and the big one today, not only the local derby between Bishop Auckland and Shildon but 1st v 2nd.

Two good footballing sides tearing up this division and going head on. Although Bishop won the away fixture at Shildon earlier this season, it's not going to be easy today and am expecting a tight game here at Heritage Park.

Bishop Auckland have been here since 2010 and prior to that were ground sharing with Spennymoor, Shildon, West Auckland, after vacating their old ground at Kingsway, before building the new ground. The driving force behind this was director Terry Jackson. The ground is actually owned by the local council on a long lease and also used by Middlesbrough U21's. The Teeside club also keep the pitch in good shape for their premiership players and the pitch and facilities here are probably the best in this division. The ground has a capacity of 2,000(but can, I'm informed, go up to 2,500). The main stand seating has 240 seats and has great views over the pitch and all around the stadium. Opposite is an uncovered walkway and behind one goal is covered terracing. The opposite goal has 2 separate sections of seating but are uncovered. The seats have been left by Darlington after they left their ground sharing here.

For this bank holiday Monday fixture they are expecting in the region of appx a 1,000 crowd. The board of the club is made up of 7 directors, including Steve Coulthard(Chairman), Catherine Pearson(Secretary), Kevin Bowker(who gave me a tour of the ground), Terry Jackson(the driving force), and Graham Wood. Kevin is responsible for getting in, and keeping, the sponsors with the club. This can be seen with the sponsors boards displayed right across the terracing opposite the main stand. They have appx 100 sponsors renewing each year at £500pa. The board members make the decisions for the club, however they also have a supporters club fan representative, alongside 250 shareholders contributing to the club anything from £100 to £5,000.

I've come across, and spoke to, David Illingworth, a Bishop fan for the past 60 years. David incidentally has the original 1939 & 1935 FA Amateur cup final programmes that Bishop were in. The 1939 programme is valued at over £800! The club are in a good healthy position going forward now, a great set of loyal fans, a great friendship with Man Utd going back to the Munich disaster of 1958, and even a museum shop in the centre of town! The museum is ably overseen by ex miner Barry, who can talk a lot and will educate you regards the club and also mining. A great character! You'll also catch Steve(Chairman) in the museum shop most days.

Players to look out for are centre forward Louis Johnson and keeper Ryan Catterick. The pitch is able to play on today, whilst a lot of other local games were being called off due to the recent deluge of rain(again!), with great thanks to the ground staff. It was a tight game with both teams defending and attacking well. 18 mins gone and Shildon strike first with a low drive into the net via no.4 David Vincent. 37 mins gone and a penalty to the away side, saved by the keeper but hooked in on the rebound from no.9 Ardelean. HT and it's 0-2 although Shildon had another disallowed for offside. Into the 2nd half and Bishops get back into the game in the 75th min. with a well placed header from no.16 Liam Henderson. Then there was a frantic last 15 mins of crosses & near misses either side of the goalposts…but in the 84th min.a cross from Kasey and a goal from Shildons no.11 Joe Posthill finishes off at 1-3

The attendance today was a fantastic 1,102 in the rainy, slippery conditions. The Bishops are the best supported team away in this division with a regular following of 60-100 every away game. The club left their previous ground to raise funds to get a grant from the football foundation, to build their new stadium, and they previously shared the ground with the cricket club.

However, it all started when theological students from Oxford and Cambridge University whilst studying at Auckland Castle, home of the bishop of Durham in Bishop Auckland; formed a team known as Bishop Auckland Church Institute in 1882. A later dispute caused a breakaway team called Auckland Town to be formed in 1886/87 and from the upheaval Bishop Auckland were formed. Club colours chosen were royal blue with white facings and subsequently the light and dark blue colours of the original church institute representing the colours of Oxbridge.

Auckland Town were founder members of the Northern league in 1889 but left after its first season before returning as Bishop Auckland in 1893. Between 1893 and 1988, the club won the League a record 19 times. The most successful period in the Northern League was 1947-1956 when the team never finished below 2nd place. They were champions seven times and runners up three times. Following the tragic Munich air crash of 1958, three of the team - Bob Hardistry, Wayne Bradley, and Derek Lewin went to assist Man Utd. Bradley became a regular in United's first team and went on to play for the full England team.

The FA Amateur Cup - Bishops record was without equal. Appearing in the final 18 times, winning ten times, including three in a row in 1955, 1956, and 1957, and semi finalists on 27 occasions. When the cup ceased in 1974, the club was presented with a replica of the trophy in recognition of its outstanding record.

1988 - almost a century after first joining the Northern League the club decided to enter the non league pyramid system via the Northern Premier League. The Bishop's would spend 18 seasons in the NPL before returning to the clubs Northern League roots in 2006.

BISHOPS STORTFORD V SOUTHEND UNITED
PRE SEASON FRIENDLY

20/07/24

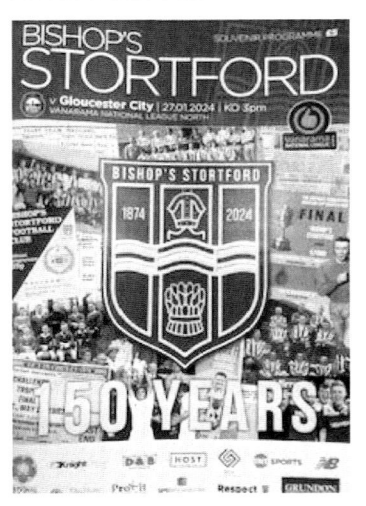

Just into Hertfordshire, from a short drive up the M11, and it's Bishops Stortford's first home friendly of the season v Southend United for this 1pm KO.

Two divisions separate the two teams now and the home side are in their familiar all blue strip, whereas the away side are in a fetching pink top & grey shorts. Recently relegated from the National League North, where they should never have been placed as there were a few other clubs in the National League that were further north than them. They lost their appeal to be placed in the National South and had a tough time financially because of this.

They have a new manager in place - Steve Castle - who only started 3 weeks ago, and was previously at St Albans as player, ass.manager, and manager, as well as Cambridge Utd, Takeley, and Royston Town, and most famously as a player at Leyton Orient.

The club have 90 youth teams which is a staggering amount and must be the biggest in the country(second only to Berkhampstead I'm informed). Stortford are looking to combine the youth and 1st team under one banner and they also have a partnership with F2 who run their education programme. The soon to be facilities here will include classrooms and a media course being run here.

Steve Smith - Majority shareholder - first came to the club 6 years ago and was also manager for the past 5 years, formerly at Heybridge Swifts & Chelmsford City. He's built the club up over the 5 years, getting them promotion, then last season relegation and having lost 11 players. Their new manager is here with a mostly new squad, a few new signings and a number of youngsters to fit in. Looking to consolidate, but compete this season.

This year the club are celebrating their 150th anniversary since their formation, so one of the older clubs still going. Secretary, Fred Plume, informs me that the club are hoping to move to a new ground within the borough - they've been here since 1999 after their move from Rhodes Avenue, they just need to reach an agreement with the local authority. Also in attendance today is a famous name in non league circles - John Still - formerly with Bishop's Stortford when they won the FA Amateur cup in 1974 v Ilford.

BLYTH SPARTANS V KINGS LYNN TOWN
NATIONAL LEAGUE NORTH

09/03/24

A short drive from SE London this morning, up to Northumberland for one of the most famous non league sides in history - the home of the mighty Blyth Spartans. Today taking on Kings Lynn Town in this bottom half of the table of the National League North.

The ground itself has a main stand sponsored by 'Port of Blyth'. This has a two tiered seating section. Opposite you have the West Side(Ferguson stand) which is covered terracing, and unusually for this level, you have two covered terraced areas, the North(Frankie Southern)and South(Lennons)stands, behind both goals. The main stand houses the dressing rooms below, along with offices, and upstairs the hospitality/sponsors/boardroom area. The club shop is located near the entrance to the park turnstiles, and the bar clubhouse is just outside the other turnstile.

The former owner - Tony Platten - has recently sold the club to local businessman Irfan Liaquat, who is bringing on board, fresh ideas, capital, and a plan to take the Spartans into the Football League for the first time. In speaking with Irfan, he is looking at investing both on and off the field. Three new players have already been bought in, more seats are planned, floodlights upgrading, another food outlet in place, and importantly finding out what the fans want and their concerns. They are also concentrating on the ladies team and highlighting the heritage with 'Wor Bella' the most famous Ladies Blyth footballer you've never heard of! Steve Howard is also in as Sports Director - ex Derby county player.

The club will be looking to increase crowd numbers and to quote Irfan - "Engagement is the key to success". There is currently a big connection with Greece due to the Spartans name.

The club were founded in 1899 by Fred Stoker(not Bram, as that would be too Draculish!) who name the club after the Greek Spartans Army in the hope that the players would give their all as they went into 'battle' on the field...so the story goes.....Blyth trot out in their resplendent green & white shirts, black shorts, green socks, whereas Kings Lynn have their unusual away kit of white top, yellow shorts, and light blue socks. Think Kings Lynn made the colours up as they went along! The game itself was an away win, yet could have been 3-1 if not for the Kings Lynn keeper and the post. An even more important game coming up on Tuesday this time v Darlington.

First chat was with Matty the media guy at the club. He feels that the new chairman is very ambitious and looking to take the club forward. The area over recent years has had a regeneration and is becoming a nice place to live. The groundsman Peter, will talk incessantly about his love of the pitch and such interesting topics as wormcasts! The manager - Jon Shaw - has got plenty of experience both as an ex professional player with the likes of Sheffield Wednesday, and managing at South Shields and Gateshead. He has his UEFA B coaching badge and currently studying for his A. As for the players, one's to look out for are Will McGowan who plays as a no.10, Nicky Deverdics(captain),Michael Liddle (left wing back), Jordan Cook, Harry Gardiner(currently on loan from Sunderland).

Former chairman Tony has been with the club 24 years now and came in initially and rescued the club to clear their then debt of £54K, but then found out later it was in actual fact a total of £144K!! If it wasn't for Tony coming in then HMRC would have wound up the club. He then set about a total renovation of the club. At that time both terraces, behind the goals, were uncovered and ash terraces. Monies raised came from the Football Stadia Improvement Fund(75%), the local authority(who owned the ground), and the chairman himself.

The new owner, Irfan Liaquat, has been successful in real estate, and deploying capital to investment trusts, also having strong business contacts in Italy and Germany. Potentially from June this year, there will be a business contract with castles in Northumberland and the football club, keen to build on the clubs heritage in its 125th anniversary year. The collaboration will see a new special edition football shirt incorporating the castles on it, which sounds, and is, unique. With regards to expansion, the club has already invested in three new players, and to follow will be - more seats, new floodlights, two food trailers with a choice of foods. The 2-5 year plan is to initially sustain the club and then strengthen, getting the community on board from all backgrounds, and increasing numbers.The club will collaborate with the 'kick it out' campaign and look to attract minority groups to the club within the community, bringing together academy sessions for all backgrounds. The community engagement will be brought into focus by Richard Kirkby, one of the new directors. The other new director - Steve Howard - is the sporting director and also overseeing the management side. So, with the history of the club going back now 125 years we can reflect on some of that.

Everyone remembers the historic record breaking FA cup run by the club in 1977-78(well at least I do myself!) when they reached the 5th round and taking Wrexham to a replay, which means they were in the 'hat' for the 6th round draw. The replay was at St James Park(their local rivals at Newcastle United!) and roared on by a crowd of over 42,000 were only narrowly defeated. It could have been Arsenal next. The crowd unofficially was over 52,000 as a barrier was broken through and another 10,000 crowded in!

Blyth and the FA cup don't stop there though. In 2009, the club were at it again. They got through to the **3rd round against Blackburn, beating** Shrewsbury and Bournemouth in the process, which paid for the North stand cover, and floodlights from the 1950's were upgraded. Come 2014 and its the 3rd round again this time v Birmingham City. **The rece**ipts from that paid **off some deb**ts.

Going back in history when the club was founded in 1899, two years later they first played in the Northumberland League, winning that League in the first season.Then joining the Northern Alliance for six seasons winning the League twice.They became semi professional in 1913 joining the North Eastern league and remained there till the League folded in 1958. Then joining the Midland League and the Northern Counties league till both those Leagues folded. By 1964 they turned amateur and joined the Northern league where they were for 29 years, winning the League title ten times and runners up five times. Promotion followed in 1994 to the Northern premier League and in their first season they won the double. Then in 2006 they won the title and promotion to the Conference North. In 2012, the club were relegated for the first time ever. In that division they reached the play off semi final in 2016 losing to Workington AFC, after finishing runners up to Darlington 1883 in the League. No messingabout the following season as they roared away amassing a total of 101 points in winning the League.

BOWERS & PITSEA V BRENTWOOD TOWN
ISTHMIAN NORTH DIVISION PLAY OFF FINAL
04/05/24

An all Essex clash between the boys in red v blue and another healthy attendance here. Bowers on the up again after getting relegated from the Isthmian Premier Division last season and aiming to come straight back up. Ably managed by top tactical manager - James Collins - who has managed numerous Kent sides in the past and has stepped across the river Thames to Essex to unchartered territory! The crowds have increased from last seasons Premier Division of appx 100 to an average now of just under 300. A massive regular increase from the wider community as far away as Southend.

The volunteers here are doing a tremendous job and they even have one of their sponsors manning the turnstiles! The clubs chairman - Barry Hubbard - a stalwart of the club over the past 24 years, informs me that the club were previously named Bowers United. They added the Pitsea to the name to attract more from the local community. The club was originally formed in 1946, after a lot of men came back from the war and wanted to start their own local football team. The previous colours here were claret and blue after the chairman's love of West Ham, and have been subsequently changed to red when Rob Small took over.

In talking with James(the tactical manager), he has been a player, winning the London Senior Cup along the way, and has managed numerous Kent sides. Starting off as reserve manager at Erith Town, 3 years under Tony Russell(currently boss at Lewes FC), then promoted to first team manager. Left to manage Sutton Athletic winning 2 cups and finishing 4th in the first season. Then onto Corinthian finishing 2nd in the league with the club having no budget, before going onto Lordswood. Cray Valley were next where he won the London Senior cup and finished 4th. Next up was Chatham Town winning 2 Kent cups and finishing 4th. Moving onto Faversham where he stayed for 3 years before pushing on higher up and 'over the water' to Bowers. James joined because the club liked his CV best. Coaching badges....he has none! He is unorthodox and hard working. He tends to look at other teams and exploits their weaknesses. No one knows his team tactics! He continually studies the game and mainly coaches the players himself with the help of his brother Alan. There are no 'star' players as they all work together as a team. James's job was made harder in his first season as all the players at the club left when he joined. He used 58 players from wherever, mostly lower divisions on a low budget, and has now built up to a promotion winning side.

The Chairman Barry Hubbard, has been with the club for 24 years now, when they were Bowers United, and were run by the social club at the time.

The ground at the time was non existent - it just had a small stand and handrails. It was built up over time with money from Michael Barnard(director).They run a Limited Company and have done well at the Stock Exchange. The money has been ploughed back into the community with youth football and having 2 ladies and 4 girls teams now. Michael has paid for all this out of his charity which has really progressed the club. This will ensure that the club will be maintained indefinitely for football and the community. He also wants to start up mental health illness help and awareness for the local kids within the community. Other help is being given to local grassroots charities such as women's refuge centre's and help in local schools.

Recent upgrades to the ground have been the 3G pitch, with constant hire as you would expect. The new sports bar and function room, alongside the solar panels which is a great economic benefit to the club, making it very sustainable.

The LED floodlights have been changed due to the cost. If the club get promoted further then more seating will be provided at the ground.

They have created a club membership of just £10p.a. Receiving discounted prices on drinks, functions etc......and the club shop shares space with the burger bar! Next time you queue up there order a quarter pounder and a fabulous mug with the club crest on.

1946 - the year the club was formed by Len Salmon, hence the name of the stadium. A club that will survive and flourish due to the charitable vision of Michael Barnard and Barry Hubbard at the helm.

The game itself - 16 mins gone and Bowers go 1-0 up through Chris Millar, with the pitch ablaze with sunshine. Matt Cripps gets a goal back for Brentwood after 34 mins, then in the second half Bowers, against the run of play, get a penalty. Those short run ups are no good as the keeper calmly saves it...and so to extra time at 1-1...and still the two sides can't be separated, so the lottery of penalties once again takes over. The Brentwood keeper gets booked before he goes up for the 2nd penalty for being stroppy and finally it's Bowers that get over the line winning 3-2 on penalties and only needed to take 4 penalties. Welcome back Bowers & Pitsea to the Isthmian Premier. Today's attendance was well over a 1,000 plus.

They are now at a stage where they don't ground share anymore - Hashtag United have moved on - and they have turned other clubs down to concentrate on their own clubs. Their charity day will generate more income and their crowds have trebled in size.

BROOK HOUSE V BELSTONE
COMBINED COUNTIES LEAGUE DIVISION 1

06/08/24

Over to Middlesex for tonight's 1st midweek competitive game of the season - Brook House v Belstone in the Combined Counties League Division 1 (step 6).

A lovely club with a nice set up and the hospitality here is second to none. A club worth visiting. Nearest tube station is Northolt and then a no.90 bus stops right outside the ground.

Speaking with Vice Chair Robbie Kettle and long standing Chair Barry Stone, they inform the club was originally formed in 1974 with the founder Billy Ball, from a merger between Charville and Hayes North. They started as a Sunday league side and came from Brook House pub. So, just celebrating their 50th anniversary this year. They have previously been up to step 4 being in the Southern League, and also formerly in the London Spartan League, when I played against them personally in the 80's for Ilford FC. The club had previously won the Isthmian League Division 3, then the non league system started to form 'steps' in the pyramid.

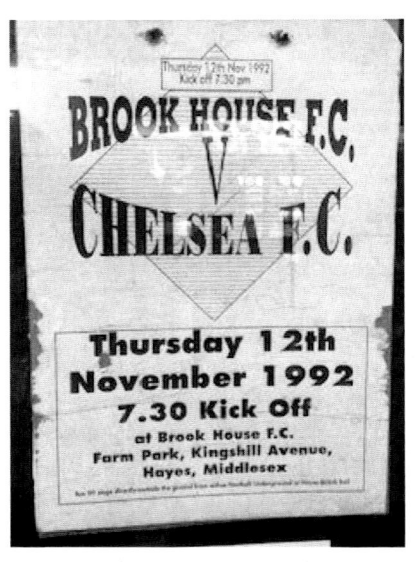

Brook House once played Chelsea (in a friendly) in 1992 to open their new floodlights. Chelsea brought down a strong side, with an attendance of over 1,000, which also helped the club financially. Last season they won the Middlesex Premier cup, which is the second most prestigious cup in Middlesex. They also won the Middlesex Senior cup in 2009 beating Hendon.

Groundwise - the pitch is grass, and they recently had a grant for the irrigation, and are about to work on the drainage(as it's collapsed!). The £90K grant for this will come from the Football Foundation/FA. Their ground is up to step 4 standard now. The money they received during covid, they wisely spent on improving the infrastructure of the ground as well as helping through financial despair. The players changing rooms were originally situated in the car park. Most of their income is derived from the bar, which is well used, and from the chairman.

The club is run as a community club and registered as a limited company, and are one of the biggest local clubs around. Their youth section is self funded and finance mainly comes from the annual weekend tournament held here, hosting 280 6-a-side teams, titled 'summer sixes'. They would love to have a disability team at the club but can't. Reason is you can't get access to the club, for wheelchairs and even buggies for children, as the council deemed it fit to erect barriers nearby to stop people getting in! This was due to joy riders on bikes scrambling around in the areas adjacent to the ground. They now have some financial help in the form of grants from the council. The club has a front and rear bar in the clubhouse(a short walk from the ground itself). Initially opened on both weekend days, it's now open every day and generates funds to make the club self sustainable.

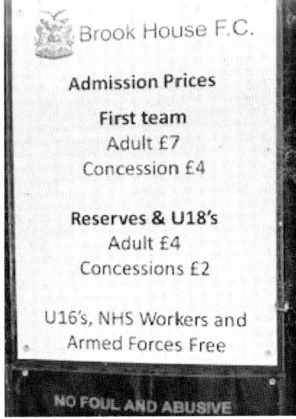

Brook House F.C.

Admission Prices

First team
Adult £7
Concession £4

Reserves & U18's
Adult £4
Concessions £2

U16's, NHS Workers and Armed Forces Free

NO FOUL AND ABUSIVE

Other sports use the clubhouse as well as parents of the youth clubs. Those youth clubs, 19 in total, are all local boys and girls, as well as having a ladies team, U18 & reserves. The club have created a pathway in which youngsters can go from U7 to the 1st team. Five of the reserves came from the U16 team last week. Sounds like the youth is the way forward for this club. One famous name who started here was Neil Shipperley(his father Dave was ex manager), who subsequently went on to Chelsea, Southampton, C.Palace, Charlton, Reading, following manager Dave Bassett around the clubs.

The scene is set for tonight's game with the new look, high powered LED floodlights - they're all the rage! - which look well designed and powerful. Brook House are in their usual home kit of blue & white stripes, blue shorts, and Belstone in red & black stripes and black shorts. We come up to HT and it's the away team who score in the 44th min. Come the second, Brook House get well on top with two goals early on. It could have been more with the chances they had but some good goalkeeping by Belstone kept them in the game. The final whistle goes then it becomes a mass brawl as no.77(yes 77!)for Belstone punches a home player in the back who goes down. Upshot is, I think 2 red cards and 2 yellows after the final whistle including the away manager…and 2-1 to Brook House! Looks like they have a good side going forward with their current manager Robert Russell, and having been in this division now for 4 years, they'll be looking to push for promotion.

Crowd tonight was in the region of 150 with 80 paying customers.

CAMBRIDGE CITY FC REVIEW
ISTHMIAN LEAGUE NORTH

26/09/24

A brand new stadium on the outskirts of a famous city, is going to be the new home of Cambridge City.

Based in the village of Sawston, and currently in the Isthmian League North division at step 4, City are an ambitious club looking to get to step 2 level.

The current capacity at the new ground, which is just about to open in November, is at 3,000. Two steps above they would look to increase to 4,000 with an added turnstile block and increased terracing.

In speaking with manager Jamie Cureton, on a rain lashed Thursday evening training session at their new ground, I get a feeling of optimism here with a club getting a balance right between winning and entertaining at the same time. Jamie has a vast amount of experience, not just a UEFA coaching B badge but playing over 1,000 games for the likes of Norwich, Bristol Rovers, Reading, QPR in the football league, and also non league with Farnborough, Bishops Stortford, St Albans City, Hornchurch. To quote Jamie in this new era for the club, "It's a perfect opportunity to build". With a brand new stadium, youth and academy section, they have aspirations of going up the leagues and it's his job to build! They're looking to be self sustainable in producing their own players. As for tactics, it's for the other teams to worry about them, especially when they play attacking football at pace.

The club were originally founded in 1908, and are nicknamed the Lilywhites for obvious reasons with their shirt colours.

Their previous ground was at Milton Road and was sold to developers in the mid 80's so that they could move on. In between they've been ground sharing with Histon FC and St Ives Town, twice with both clubs. They were in financial difficulties during those times but have since turned things around, and under the leadership of Chairman Kevin Satchell, and general manager Alice Dewey, the club are on the up and looking ahead to a bright future.

They have a great set of volunteers - a key band of 20 where they have a regular working party every Wednesday to work on the ground.

The new cafe will be open Monday to Friday from morning to evening for local villagers as a real hub for the community. They even propose to set up weekend nights with entertainment including a Northern soul night.

The club work closely with the local community, especially with schools, and have a supporters trust which meets at the local pub. For charitable work they include fun runs.

Their average crowds at their ground share have been around 200, which they are looking to double when they play at their new home.

As for their youth, they have both boys & girls teams from U12 to U18's, as well as a ladies team. For the academy they will have rooms for their education and a 3g pitch for those 16-18 year olds.

The new ground has taken awhile over the years to get to this stage of about to play at the new stadium. They first bought land in this village from a developer who was originally going to build houses. The club needed to get planning permission, not that easy when its on green belt land and the neighbour's didn't like the thought of their houses being devalued! The neighbour's objected to the process, it went to judicial review, and the neighbour's won on an appeal.

South Cambridgeshire authority said to the club to put through again, and they finally won with planning permission granted.The work started in early 2021 using a number of different contractors.

When it came to the dressing rooms, the club crowd funded for this and raised £30K, with another £10K coming from the Sport Foundation.There are also 3 portakabins going to provide for - the refs room, medical room(for players & fans), and toilets.

Overall this is a family run club with secretary Andy Dewey being a volunteer for 50 years now. His daughter Alice (general manager), has been coming to the club with her Dad since the age of 2.

Like most clubs now there is a pathway from youth to first team, with the likes of Ed Tassell, a defender who is nearly 18, making that grade. Three of their most famous players being - Neil Harris, former player & manager at Millwall whom they sold to for £100K, including add ons, Vic Watson, former West Ham and England international, and Michael Gash who went on to manage Peterborough Sports.

They do have a club shop at the new building, but their current one is being driven to and from St Ives (the ground share) each match day! Other income streams will be from their new hospitality suite, four other boxes(which are also used during the week), and a potential restaurant for the future.

CHESHAM UNITED V BRAINTREE TOWN
FA CUP 4TH QUALIFYING ROUND REPLAY

17/20/23

FA cup 4th qualifying round replay, and over to Buckinghamshire for Chesham United v Braintree Town.

Bucks v Essex and Maidstone United await the winners in the 1st round proper.

This club, and ground, is full of history and quirkiness which you'll have to see to believe. I'll tell you later!

However, the home team play in claret & blue - what's not to like!

Crowd favourite songs tonight seem to be 'We are those bast***s in claret and blue', 'He's got a pineapple on his head' and 'We're going to Wembley' - I do so admire their optimism!

0-1 to Braintree at HT after a fluke deflection. Attendance is officially 826, and at least 4 dogs with club colours on!....into 4 mins added time at the end and Chesham get a last gasp equaliser.

So, we go into extra time. The Chesham fans swap ends for the first half of extra time. The away fans don't. Interesting. Then, Lucas Sinclair slots in for the 2nd. The home crowd go wild. The away fans understandably don't!...we then have 3 added mins at the end of extra time. Braintree pushing up, including their goalkeeper who goes AWOL, when Chesham counterattack on the break, skip past the keeper and defende,r and pass into the net to send Chesham through to the 1st round(first time since 2016).

Going back a few years - before the 1st world war- there were two teams. Chesham Generals and Chesham Town. Post WW1 they formed into one club - Chesham United - as half the players on both sides were killed during the war. They originally played on the cricket pitch until moving to the present ground, next door, in 1931.

They uniquely are the only ground to have 'tank traps' buried on the terraces behind the goal. This was to stop Hitlers panzer division from marauding across the country in case of invasion! The main stand was literally transported through the town from a previous ground and placed here. It was re built in 1981 after a fire destroyed the original. The clubhouse was rescued from RAF Halton, the turnstiles and gate from the Old Den at Millwall, and would you believe a number of former players(obviously no longer with the club!)ashes are buried underneath the pitch!

Their most famous day was when they were in the FA Amateur cup final in 1968 against Leytonstone. That day they took 25,000 fans to Wembley. Literally the whole town was emptied and silent for the day.

Good luck to Chesham in the next round and great meeting up with Giles - the club shop man, Mike the Secretary, Ray the tea man/hospitality, and Peter the Chairman.

CRAY WANDERERS V CRYSTAL PALACE
PRE SEASON FRIENDLY

26/07/24

Cray Wanderers have been ground sharing with Bromley for the past 20 years and have just moved into their new revamped stadium over at Flamingo Park off the A20.

They are currently at step 3 and play in the Isthmian Premier Division.

The club are the oldest in London and the second oldest football association club in the world (before Hallam FC), formed back in 1860, when migrant workers building the Cray Valley viaduct teamed up with villagers from St Mary Cray.

Nowadays they have 30 youth teams, and girls teams, from U7's(3 teams at this level) up to seniors representing this established club, and a new academy side.

It was nice meeting up with Director & CEO Sam Wright who filled me in on plans for the new ground.

Cray Wanderers have been in exile from the Crays since 1973 when they lost the Grassmeade ground in Chelsfield Road due to housing development. They moved to Oxford Road, on the borders of Footscray and Sidcup but when that ground became unsuitable for step 5 football(they were playing in the Kent League), they moved to Bromley's ground.

March 2018 - Bromley Council approved a new football stadium/community hub at Flamingo Park in Sidcup, and the green light was given with approval by the GLA(Greater London Authority). 2018/19 - The Wanderers were now playing in the newly formed Isthmian South East Division and were the first Champions, and have reached 5th place in the Isthmian Premier.

Now, the real origins of Cray Wanderers are linked to the construction of the London, Chatham and Dover railway line during 1858 to 1860. During their leisure time, migrant workers kicked a ball around, and that is how the club originated in the St Mary Cray village. The pitch at Star lane is now a cemetery, and is located beneath the nine arch railway viaduct that spans the Cray Valley. The industrial belt of the River Cray, especially the paper mills, provided much of the clubs support up till the 1950's.

They had a spell as a professional club from 1985, of which they were a nursery club for Woolwich Arsenal during part of this period. They were one of the founder members of the Kent League in 1894/95 and won the League in 1901/02.

After WW1 Cray switched to the London League until 1934. They rejoined the Kent League in 1934/35 where they remained for 4 years due to the loss of their Fordcroft ground in Cray Avenue, their home since 1898. The club were forced to go down to a lower level of football, and various temporary grounds, and struggling in the South London Alliance and Kent Amateur league.

1951/52 - they regained their London League and senior status, then moving to a new ground in Grassmeade in 1955. This was a successful period drawing on support from the Orpington area and playing in the Aetolian League winning the League three times, the League cup twice, and the Kent Amateur cup three times. They then switched to the semi professional Metropolitan League in 1966/67. In 1971/72 a merger of the Metropolitan League and The Greater London League created the Met London League. Cray moved to Oxford Road in 1973/74 at that stadium winning the London Spartan League in both 1976/77 & 1977/78. Cray decided to return to the Kent League in 1978/79 and won the League in 1980/81.

The new club chairman - Gary Hillman - arrived in 1994/95 and by the late 90's Cray had arrived at the Bromley ground as tenants. Now into a new era with their own ground, with a new seated stand, looking resplendent in team colours of yellow and black. There are also 2 blocks of 2 turnstiles (4 in total) at 2 different entrances, a fan zone in front of the clubhouse, a new bar/kitchen with easy access for fans during the game, a club shop well stocked with merchandise including wall to wall history of the club all around. The surface has recently been laid where the picnic benches are, with steps out up to the bar. Disability ramps are well placed to both the bar area and up to the main stand. The next phase will be the wood to be replaced, and strengthened, to the upstairs balcony to be able to use. This will have a fantastic view higher up of the ground.

The ground is on the borders of three different areas, namely Chislehurst, Sidcup, New Eltham - which covers three London Boroughs of Bromley, Bexley, and Greenwich.

The CEO is looking at getting in crowds of around 1,000, whereas their recent tenure at Bromley FC had crowds of appx 250.

The game itself against a Premiership U18 team was a real tough test, who were a bit of a class act tonight. A good test though and a fantastic crowd of 707 for a friendly.

CROCKENHILL V FLEETDOWN UNITED RESERVES
KENT COUNTY LEAGUE DIVISION 2 WEST

02/09/23

Over to Crockenhill FC today - J3 M25 - for a serious Kent County League Division 2 West game v Fleetdown United reserves.

Some of you may know this ground as the film set for 'The Bromley boys'. Yes, it's on Netflix - do check it out! Recognise the main stand from the film.

Do check out this ground as it has much originality about it and certainly history. They don't charge admission to get in, because at this level, with the Kent FA, they're not allowed to! If they did, then you would come across(and through) the original turnstiles over a 100 years old from Charlton Athletic.

The main clubhouse, with bar, food facilities, tv, also doubles up at what looks like a football museum with scarves, pennants, team photos, newspaper cuttings.

This clubhouse was formerly turned into an army barracks and had beds on either side where the table and chairs are currently situated. The army were billeted here during the war, the pitch concreted over, and a gunner situated on the pitch to fire upon any German planes high above...and they used to shoot them down from behind!

So, to the football. Well, they've gone through two consecutive relegations - from Premier Division to Division 2. The positive side is that they can't go any lower!

Not expecting too much, they surprised me, and themselves, by going into a 2-0 lead at half time. Ginger number 14 scored a great goal direct from a free kick, for the second, and celebrated like it was the best goal he'd ever scored. They also have a noisy centre forward who looked no taller than myself, bald and bearded looking like he runs a Turkish barbers, and eaten all the kebabs from last night! The lino's today were a chap who had a t shirt on and long shorts looking like he'd just come back from a beach holiday, and the home side was one of the subs! Probably the lowest level of football I've seen since the RAF last shot the Germans down over the Kent countryside.

Had a great chat with the chairman Steve Cullen along with another official Peter Jewell - a diamond geezer giving a great detailed history of the club and stories too many to tell and some unprintable

Second half kicks off and would you Adam and Eve it the opposition score two quick goals one after the after. 5 minutes later they get a third after the keeper failed to keep out the cross and it sails into the net. Unfortunately the score stayed that way and Fleetdown came away with a 3-2 away win.

This is a must go to ground. The volunteers and owners of the club really make it and of course keep it ticking over and great hospitality awaits.

The club incidentally was formed earlier before the war, then disbanded at the start of the war in 1939, as the army took over and concreted the pitch. Then reformed again after the war in 1946.

Their most famous player bring Tony Cascarino before pursuing his career further with Gillingham, then Millwall.

CROOK TOWN V HOLKER OLD BOYS
FA VASE 2ND QUALIFYING ROUND

21/09/24

Saving one of the best grounds till last on my adventures for THE BEAUTIFUL GROUNDS 2 - and it's up to County Durham for Crook Town AFC.

This afternoon they host Holker Old Boys(from the Barrow area)in this FA Vase 2nd Qualifying round. Crook are currently 8th in the table of the Northern League Division 1 at step 5 level, whilst Holker are a step 6 side. The warmth and friendliness at this club is second to none, and overseeing all this is one of the youngest football chairman around, and the youngest chairman in the clubs history, Chris McDonald at age 35.

Chris has only been at the helm now for 3 months(although was previously secretary for 7 years)and already has rapidly improved areas of the stadium such as the clubhouse which was refurbed inside and out, club shop(reclaimed 2nd turnstile with the turnstile still intact there), giving more access for mobility, more concrete hard standing all around, and hand rails. There is a prominent food area named "only foods and sauces" which sells the speciality black and amber burger - which is black pudding, bacon, cheese burger.

They have a 'Crook Fest' held here annually at the ground on the first May day bank holiday. Plenty of live bands, DJ's, with 3 marquees and a beer tent. They get a crowd of around 2,000 and is their main fund raiser of the year. Chris is a very forward thinking chairman and aside from transforming the merchandise area with plenty of stock available, including favourite player T shirts such as "Moody's on fire", he is also planning a non league football dogs day where you can all come along with your dogs(bring a stray if you haven't got one!)and enjoy the experience along with your dog. You'll be 'barking mad' not to!

They have currently 9 youth teams, having a pathway from youth to the first team. A great example of this is current player Charlie Bunton who has played through every level at the club and now has 5 goals for the first team.

A previous famous player - Jimmy McMillan - has had the bar named after him! He incidentally played in two of the Amateur cup winning sides, of which the club have won 5 in total. The cup that was on display here today, affectionately known as the Barcelona cup, is a trophy played between the 2 teams between 1913-1922 as the Herbert Hutchison memorial.

The club were originally founded in 1889, from a merger between Crook FC and Crook Excelsior. Their home ground Millfield, belonged to the rugby ground at the time. It is now owned by the local council with 92 years left on the lease. The new stand was built in 1926 and still stands today nearly 100 years on. This was at a cost of £1,300. Waste from the local coal mines was deposited around all sides of the ground to form grass banks as you can see today.

The period of 1955-1965 was the most successful in the clubs history, recognised as one of the best clubs in the country at the time. In 1955 they drew with Derby in the FA cup. During the game, former England centre forward, Jesse Pye, rocketed a 30 yard shot off the crossbar. The crossbar had to be replaced after the game as it had cracked! It's still kept under the main stand to this day.

In 1957, a game v Bishop Auckland had a crowd of 27,000. These were the two top teams in the country(albeit amateur)at the time.

One of Barcelona's greatest ever managers(and longest serving) was Jack Greenwell. He joined Crook at age 17 whilst working down the mines 6 days a week. He guested for West Auckland when they won the first world cup in 1909.

He then joined Barcelona in 1912, and was the first manager to play out from the back passing(it'll never catch on!). Moving to Espanol in 1928, Valencia, Sporting Gijon, Real Sociedad, and even managed the Peruvian national team. He is revered in Barcelona, and on the club shirt the badge has an England flag as part of it in memory of him. He can also be found in Barclays Bank, Crook High Street, where he is immortalised in a blue placque in a hall of fame.

Expansion plans in the offing are to build a mobility area to allow for greater inclusion. This is situated near one of the corner flags, currently a hard standing area and will be covered. To quote 'Will modernise the ground yet keep the history'.

The club are at their highest position ever and have recently gone to the furthest in the FA cup - so far. If they win promotion to the next step, then they would need to reinstate the 2nd turnstile, infill all barriers surrounding the pitch at a cost of £45/60K, and erect a 6' fence behind the goal and in front of the houses behind the far goal.

This is a real caring community club, reaching out to local care homes for those who can't get to football normally. They come in via their carers who all get free admission. They also hold charity days with their principal charity LMA (from a young girl who died of cancer) and raised funds to get a heart monitor for a local doctors surgery. They're all inclusive in bringing young kids into the fold here, rather than them not being part of the club, and have also been a great advocate for the kick it out equality status. Local schoolchildren are encouraged to come along to games with the potential to be mascots on match days.

The average crowd here is 325 which has increased over the past couple of years, and with a total capacity of 1,500.

As for the game, it seemed a fairly even match with no goals whereas the second half Crook totally dominated having around 7/8 good chances they could have put away, mostly going over the bar. So, straight to penalties with no extra time in this cup game. The first two Holker penalties were saved by top keeper Alex Curran. This paved the way for a 4-2 win on pens.and another step closer to Wembley!

A club you will remember fondly once you've been there, so no excuse for not going now!

CURZON ASHTON V BARNET

FA CUP 1ST ROUND

04/11/23

FA Cup 1st round and it's up to Tameside in Greater Manchester to see the mighty Curzon Ashton take on the bees of Barnet.

National League North v 2nd top of the National League. Curzon are a side, steered in the right direction and on a tight budget, by chairman Wayne Salkeld. His son Jack is assistant first team manager, and daughter works behind the bar.

Formed in 1963, they've come up through the leagues to their highest position in this league by working within their means. A chairman that has brought in a number of sponsors, to help sustain this club, and are currently higher than all of their local, and more established, competitors.

Despite the stormy wet conditions around the country, this game is on with the most perfect grass pitch I've seen. All credit to the groundsman Justin Pickering. They currently have 42 teams from U/6 to U/18, also competing in the East Manchester league - the biggest junior league in the whole of the UK, so I've been told.

The clubs success has been in sustaining itself in the National League North for the last 9 consecutive seasons. The Chairman has risen through the ranks from youth team manager right up till now running the club.

So out come the players on the pitch to the strains of the Clash's 'Rock the casbah'. The mascot is a weird concoction between Superman and Elvis Presley! I know, don't ask. Curzon in their familiar all blue kit and Barnet in all white with navy stripes.

16 mins and 1-0 to Barnet with a flying header in from their centre forward.

Barnet seem to be the more controlled side with their passing going forward. Ashton have had a couple of good chances, and then a second yellow for a Barnet defender and he's off! Two more good chances come the way of the home side but not taken.

Second half and it's 0-1 and 11 v 10.

Barnet contrive to grind out a win and no upset today and Ashton had a goal disallowed nearer the end of the game. A fair result would have been a draw at least.

However, what I have come across is a club that has a real family feel about it. A great close knit community club that are increasing their attendances by 13% and superb hospitality. Nice also meeting vice chair James Newell(his son Oliver is matchday announcer), Paul McHugh the commercial manager, Rob Hurst the secretary, and chairman of local opposition club at Mossley FC Steven Porter, and not forgetting the founder of Curzon Ashton - Harry Twamley.

Celebrity spotted there was ex West Ham player Trevor Sinclair. A club well worth visiting. #UTN (up the Nash!)

DIDCOT TOWN V OXFORD CITY
PRE SEASON FRIENDLY
09/07/24

Over to Oxfordshire for tonight's 7:30pm friendly between Didcot Town and Oxford City.

Here at Loop Meadow where Secretary Paul Chalk, whom I met last season for an away game v AFC Totton, gives me the rundown on the club. This is a Trustee driven club, governed by 5 trustees. No one owns the club as it's a non profit entity and any profit made goes into the infrastructure to keep the club sustainable.

The club have now been placed into the Southern League Division 1 South, after last seasons relegation. This is going to prove a logistical challenge with the travelling involved. A lot of clubs in this division are unknown to Didcot but they should finish at least in the top 10 if not in the play offs. They have a squad of 24 with 8 of those in the development squad and under 20 years of age. A real good mix of experience and youth.

The club were originally formed in 1907 but have currently been at their present ground since 1999. They sold their previous ground, about 3/4 of a mile away, to developers and have taken on their present land of 14 acres which also includes the leisure facilities built for the council. During the covid years of 2020/22, the grants from the government were a lifeline to this club to keep going, otherwise they would have gone under. They have amazing facilities here and are currently 'trying to re energise their club'. The club has 28 youth teams from U6 to U18, so plenty of promise there for the future. In fact their current manager Jamie Heapy, came through from the boys team, as it was then, to the 1st team and has amassed an amazing 960 appearances for the club. No mean feat there! He also played in the same first team for Didcot as his father at the same time, at age 16, and his father was in his late 30's. A legend here at the club and I'm sure a stand will be named in his honour some time in the future! He was also captain of the team in 2005 when they beat AFC Sudbury 3-2 in the FA Vase final, played at White Hart Lane.

The ground has a nice old style feel to it and behind one goal you have two small seated stands on either side of the larger covered terrace - painted in red and white stripes with the club initials on. Behind the other goal is an open walk way. The main stand is on a raised level and adjacent to this you have the 'Shed'. Though not exactly Stamford Bridge, it provides cover for those to come out of the clubhouse and watch the game on 'pub' picnic benches. The clubs pitch measures up at 107 x 67 yards and is one of the longest pitches around, described as 'huge'. The current crop of players to look out for are goalkeeper Leigh Bedwell. Leigh also played for Swindon coming on as sub in a game, after Paolo Di Canio had an argument with his keeper at the time and put Leigh on instead! Centre back Luke Carnell(ex Oxford Utd.), and 18 year old youngster, and midfielder, Owen Smith…..into the second half of the game and Oxford city are 4-0 up from the first with a cracking strike from No.7 who is trialist F!,..and it's now 5-2 up to the away side as the freight trains go thundering past one goal as Didcot score! This is a stern test for Didcot this evening, as they play opponents two divisions higher, in their quest for promotion this season.....and did you know that when they played Exeter City in an FA cup game, Olly Watkins came on as a sub!

FARNHAM TOWN V JERSEY BULLS
COMBINED COUNTIES PREMIER DIVISION

27/02/24

A short journey tonight, only 1 hour 15, round to Surrey via the A2/M25/A3/A31. Tonight it's a top table clash between Farnham Town v Jersey Bulls in this Combined Counties Premier Division South. Surrey v the Channel Islands(part of)no less.

The club colours, and style, on both clubs looks like it's a Premiership clash between West Ham and Crystal Palace! Farnham Town is a club you'll be hearing more of as time goes on. Speaking with one of the directors, Frankie Hobbs, they are looking at getting back to back promotions comfortably and plans to move further up to the National League South, after eventual consolidation.

The crowds are increasing rapidly with average crowds of 550 now (was 210 only 2 years ago). They are investing heavily in all different areas, from the current squad, the junior section with over 1,000 kids and 80 teams…yes 80!, and importantly the infrastructure going forward. They plan to be ahead of any ground grading requirements each promotion they intend to get. Their committee is now, age wise, very young, with successful businessmen like Harry Hugo and Ed Kelsing coming in to push the club forward, in so many different ways.

In speaking with new chairman Harry Hugo, they have identified areas in which to build upon. The focus is on the infrastructure and also the fans experience. They want to build a legacy first They are investing in players to get success on the field, with a very good manager at the helm - Paul Johnson - they are certainly doing that this season. The club have bought in players from higher based clubs, and they are creating a winning culture, both on and off the field, making it an exciting place to come and play football. This in turn attracts more players and fans of course. Harry is seeking to build a community around the area he grew up in and the club he played for as a youngster. Its all about engagement 7 days a week . Creating a philosophy of good football, good food, and a fun place to be at.

They are also ahead of the game when it comes down to filming, the media, creating content online. The game is immediately sent onto you tube, giving you different angles of the goals throughout the game. They will also provide online characters and personalities within the club to keep the youngsters attention, making them, the club, totally transparent and media savvy. To quote - "Making people feel something".

The 5 year term plan is to achieve the highest level that Farnham can go in its history. They are looking to do right by the club and community and build a solid base at step 3 which will be self sustainable. Not withstanding making it the best ground in the country for its level. They also have on board, as a sponsor, KSI, a rapper, and a you tube group of 7, with a following of over 70 million. They sponsor the club under the name of 'Sides'(fried chicken food!) . Another company - Pitchside - sponsor the away kit. They regularly run 'Non league diaries' on You Tube, giving interviews with Harry and also the manager Paul.

Other long standing volunteers on the night were Barbara Fripp in hospitality who has been with the club over 40 years. Roger King, the chatty matchday secretary. Then there is Paul Tanner, who has been player, manager, chairman and now director of football over the past 30/40 years.

So we go in at HT at 0-0, which sounds familiar these days. Two good footballing sides but Farnham piling on the pressure more so, in this second half, something has to give....and Farnham have just hit the bar!...then in the 86th minute, a penalty to Farnham as the player is tripped in the box as he surges forward. Jersey no.3 is yellow carded for the 2nd time and gets his marching orders. The penalty is duly dispatched into the corner of the net to a happy crowd and the delirious players! This amazingly is a side that is unbeaten this season in the league. In fact after tonight it's played 24, won 24, points 72, with a goal difference of +76. With 14 games to go they could potentially finish on a maximum of 114 points.

This is some going and a massive achievement.

The ground itself has a main covered stand with seating. A bit further down is sectioned off as another new covered stand is being built with terracing only. The opposite side you have the dug outs and players tunnel, a covered old stand and a walkway going up to a slope. Behind one goal is a steep bank. Partly sectioned off as it's a no go area these days with grass banks. One side is a covered seating area, with the other side of the goal posts an open walkway. The club shop/outside bar, where you can buy beer on tap and a scarf at the same time!, is alongside the main stand at the side of the corner flag, and next to the food stall. There is also another food stall named as a 'Mystery kitchen'. They have a different dish each match day, and no one knows what it is till the day. So, an alternative to the usual burger & chips, and keeps the fans guessing!

Their current home - The Memorial Ground - holds 1,500, which they are looking to increase. However, they go back to 1906 when they were first formed. This was a merger between Farnham Bungs(the Brewery, and the first known bungs in football!)and Farnham Star. They entered the Surrey Intermediate League of which they were title winners in 1930 and 1931. They changed to the Surrey Senior League in 1947 and in the 60's the club had three succesive title wins in 1966, 67, and 68. Runners up in 1970 & 1971, before joining the Spartan league of that year. In 1975 the League merged to become the London Spartan League and the club were **placed** in **Division 1**, which **later became** the **Premier** Division in 1977. 1980 - the club transferred to the Combined Counties League, winning the title in 1992 after runners up 4 years earlier. The following season they retained their title and won **2 cups th**at season. A might**y t**reble **was h**ad. 2003 - they became members of **t**he Premier Division. 2007 - They won Division 1 but failed to get promotion due to ground grading. 2011 - promoted back to the Premier Division and relegated in 2018. 2021 - promoted to the Premier Division based on results in the abandoned 'covid' seasons. Then last season they won the League cup beating Balham in the final.

GAINSBOROUGH TRINITY V WHITBY TOWN
NORTHERN PREMIER LEAGUE PREMIER DIVISION

02/03/24

You would have thought I'd give it a miss today with all this torrential rain, and potential waterlogged pitches. NO is the answer, as Gainsborough Trinity have only had 1 game called off in the last 7 years. So, today it's Lincolnshire v North Yorkshire, with the away team being, once again, Whitby Town. This is the Northern Premier League Premier Division no less.

Speaking with Secretary - Matt Boles - the club have recently changed Chairman this season and officially appointed Andy Ward from January. They are looking to generate more money in order to make the club self sufficient with new ideas. Matt has been working with the club for the past 11 years and previously Secretary (as well as volunteering at the bar and selling programmes prior to that). Jon Wood - the groundsman - deserves a mention getting the ground in tip top condition despite the deluge of rain of late. Jon has been at the club since a kid and over 40 years. The club have invested £2,500 in a cover, for part of the pitch, which helps with the frost. The drainage system here is second to none and the water drains off really well.

The club celebrated its 150th anniversary last year and the ground is the oldest single used ground in the country according to their plaques on the wall. A great marketing piece there!

10 mins. gone and it's no.10 Declan Howe who is first on the score sheet to make it 1-0 to Gainsborough. Shortly after they also have a goal disallowed for offside, but it was a great passing move. 34 mins and it is now 2-0 with that man Howe scoring again. Come the second half Gainsborough are even more on top, with lots of pressure and passing, and it looks like Whitby have forgotten to turn up! Howe was a thorn in their side all afternoon and the surprise was that the scoreline stayed at 2-0.

The players at the club, as you would expect, are semi professional. The club have a Foundation, within the community, which helps with local events. They've also set up a PE programme within local schools. There are currently no plans for expansion, which is unusual in speaking to most clubs. If the club get promotion to the National League North then there is no new ground grading required as they are already there. The ground is actually owned by the supporters club and they regularly have the Lincolnshire county darts taking place at the clubhouse on the day of the game!

Their function room is quite large so can accommodate these tournaments. Just off this function room you have the sponsors lounge, 50 in today, so packed out including a number down from Whitby Town. The club has a junior section from ages 6-21 which also includes girls/ladies. The Foundation, their charity, took over the local sports ground. They received funding of 2M to get a new 3g pitch, which came from the Football Foundation and also the Lincolnshire FA. The Foundation employ 15 people and have been established over 10 years now. The projects they deliver on are health and wellbeing - which generates own income and is non profit making. The staff from the football club also help with this.

The club have a history going back over 150 years now. Man Utd's very first opponents were Gainsborough, and ironically their last ever game as Newton Heath was against Gainsborough! The club are known as the Holy Blues, and adding the name Trinity after their first name gives it a very religious connotation. The club was actually formed by the local reverend and started life as Trinity Recreationalists.

They have a 3 year plan in which to get back to the National League North. Including in this would be any FA cup runs to help with finance - that's a given then! They are investing in the infrastructure of the club which is in the squad of players, and in the area scouting for raw talent. Also investing in a strength and conditioning coach, using a GPS system. This tracks three main characteristics of speed distance and intensity. Not forgetting developing their own youth.

The owners and main directors - Andy Ward, Dave Horsley, and John Myskiw, oversee the running of the club and own the club equally. You also have Jed Hallam and Clare Snow, both directors, who volunteer their services working in the club shop. Jed I first came across one midweek game away at Matlock Town. Not forgetting head steward Jason Ollerton another volunteer stalwart of the club. The crowds have gone down from 1,000 last year, when they were in the play offs, to an average now of around 600. It just goes to show that success brings the crowds in like nothing else. Their most famous name seems to have been Neil Warnock who was a player/manager with the club.

Their match day printed programme is a glossy affair, which also contains interviews with the head steward, and also unusually so with the strength and conditioning coach. Far better reading than the usual boring match reviews that you get at other clubs.....oh, and today's attendance was 533.

GREAT YARMOUTH V WIVENHOE TOWN
EASTERN COUNTIES LEAGUE DIVISION 1 NORTH

17/04/24

The club were formed in 1897 although their stand pre-dates the club by 5 years - making it the oldest stand in continuous use in the entire world.

Most of the players were drawn from two very successful local sides Yarmouth Fearnought and Yarmouth Royal Artillery - very empire led then! The stand is a real piece of Victorian grandeur painted green, and is looked after by the local authority as its a listed building, but the ground isn't(listed that is).

Trees and plants are all around the ground making it picturesque, and its shares usage with the athletics club with the stand overlooking the running track.

Opposite the main stand is a covered wooden terraced stand running the length of the pitch and behind the goals are both open to the elements and surrounded by the running track.

In 1885 the council proposed 7 1/2 acres of the North Denes to be set apart as a recreation ground. The Wellesley Recreation Ground was opened on 6th August

1888(a bank holiday)by the Town Mayor, with an estimated crowd of 3,000 paying 1/- each(5p) to watch various races. Initially temporary grandstands or marquees were erected when required, but there was a need for a grandstand. A strip of land was therefore added to the Recreation Ground from vacant plots facing Marine Parade to accommodate the building of the grandstand. In 1891, a committee of the council recommended the erection of a grandstand, dressing room and refreshment pavillion at a cost of £1,000. This grandstand was opened on Whit Monday, 11th June 1892, when a combined Athletic and Cycle sports meeting was held with a crowd of 4,200.

The Wellesley Recreation Ground is now the home of Great Yarmouth FC, affectionally known as the Bloaters. It wasn't until the 1901/02 season that the club were granted permission to use the ground for home games, having spent its early seasons on the Beaconsfield playing fields.

In 1923 the club suggested the concrete steps in front of the grandstand were constructed with a toilet behind the stand. A 'pay box' and turnstile were erected(in Wellesley Road itself) and in 1924 a concrete bath was installed in the dressing rooms.

During WW2 baseball was played here with the American servicemen based nearby, while at the end of the war a thanksgiving service was held followed soon after that month by a Victory sports meeting. In 1951 repairs were carried out and was also re roofed in corrugated asbestos sheeting. Not today it wouldn't have!

The highest crowd ever there was in 1953 when in the FA cup 1st round the club took on Crystal Palace, winning 1-0, with a crowd of 8,944. Additional terracing was provided by fish boxes behind the South goal!

In 1967 a fire broke out gutting the treatment room and adjoining dressing rooms. Part of the stand remained usable but the teams had to change in the Bowls pavilion until repaired.

1982 saw the grandstand refreshment rooms converted to storage space. The part used by the football club became a hospitality lounge for entertaining visiting officials. Then in 1992, the building to the North side of the stand became a tea hut for spectators. Earlier in 1985 the grandstand was closed(due to the Bradford fire disaster)until all rubbish had been removed, no smoking signs erected and safety stewards now appeared on match days. Fire resistant linings were added to the mainly wooden grandstand. To this day announcements are made informing spectators of the smoking ban.

English Heritage were commissioned to produce a report by getting a surveyor to inspect the buildings. In May 2000 the Secretary of state decided to list the buildings, judged to be of special architectural and historic interest as Grade 2 listed.

So, to the present and the club are on the verge of getting promoted up to step 5, winning their next two games, as they have two games in hand over top placed club Framlingham Town at present. Early on Wivenhoe go 1-0 up and then on 28 mins a Louie Duffield header, from a corner, make its 1-1 then the rain lashes down. The away team take the lead again 1-2 on the stroke of HT after all the attacking from the home side. What I do see though is a youthful side full of passing and attacking flair. They are soon back on level terms 2-2 with a well taken crisp shot. Then they hit the post with another cross...so many chances now, until a penalty for the home side. Its coolly slotted home, the away manager is not happy though, gets a 2nd yellow card for his disputes, and is off. This is soon followed by another great cross and its 4-2. Top of the league with a game in hand and the crowd go wild! Well, when I say wild, the crowd is 189 which is far more than Gorleston(two divisions higher)get as they ground share here.

The club are in good shape with 20 youth teams and another 3 to be added next season, including ladies and girls teams.They also have a 9 a side 3G pitch at the end of the South goal for training, which is mostly for youth teams.

They have the lowest budget in the league so its the youth players that are pushing the club forward, plus the tactical awareness of joint managers Ryan Honeyman and Paul Blissett who are well organised. The secretary, Eden Rudling, explains that the club are looking to spend £50K on a new grass pitch(along with Gorleston FC), which should alleviate the postponements.

Many thanks to Martin Baxter for his historical research on the grandstand.

HADLEY V AYLESBURY UNITED
SOUTHERN LEAGUE DIVISION 1 CENTRAL

01/10/24

Step 4 tonight on a rainy night in North London and it's a top of the table clash, 1st v 4th, in the Southern League Division 1 Central. Hadley FC v Aylesbury United, with the home team undefeated and in their highest ever position at this level - with the lowest budget in the league.

A real family club here run by Chairman Steve Gray, President Tristan Smith, and a young manager - Anthony Clark - at the helm who seem to be taking the club places. As Anthony would say "a club run on purity and morals", which sounds refreshing. The team have been gelled, and brought up, together from a young age over the past 7 years and excelling now with the oldest player here only 25.

This is an impressive little ground with a really friendly set up and is in actual fact the only club playing in Barnet - highest ranked and oldest club I've been informed. The ground itself has a total at present of 150 seats. A main stand with covered seating at one side, seats behind one length of the ground and the other goal covered terracing. The other length you also have covered terracing. Facilities near the main stand is a typical cafe style food and drink bar with the main clubhouse outside the turnstiles in the Pavillion.

The capacity is around 1500/2000 and the biggest attendance was in 2021 for the FA cup 2nd Qualifying round replay v Enfield Town with appx 400. Their average crowds now have increased to 160/200. If, and when, they achieve promotion to step 3, then they would need to increase their seating to around 250/300.

Any expansion plans take time and it's difficult to even erect a sign stating where the club is due to one local neighbour who objects to everything!

Despite this, new dressing rooms will be built and placed nearer the pitch, and they will extend the Pavillion to form a separate bar.

Their main stand, and the one behind the goal, have been named which isn't unusual. They are named respectively, after Peter Gray(the present Chairman's grandfather), and Frank Gray. A distant relative put up some money and wanted the stand named after his father. Even in hospitality you have Kate Gray(the Chairman's mother!) continuing with the family feel to the club.

Their fans sing throughout the game with one of their faves - 'We don't need no Tottenham Hotspur, we don't need no Arse-en-al,.........all in all we're just the best team in football!'(sung to Pink Floyd's 'Another brick in the wall'), and of course - 'E I E I E I O, up the Southern League Division 1 Central we go, when we get promotion, this is what we sing, we are Hadley, we are Hadley, Clarky is our king!' You can even buy tennis balls off a fan who goes round selling them for a £1 a go. You then get to throw them onto the pitch - at HT that is, not during the game! - and the winner is the one nearest the centre circle for a cash prize! Beats a first goal, 50/50 draw any day.

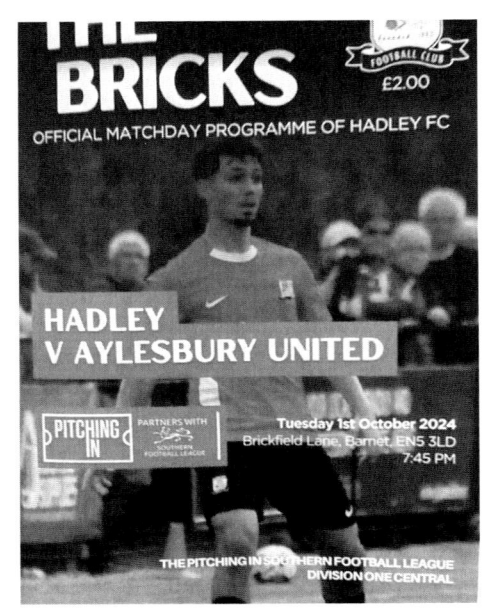

They also produce a neat **little**, and **informative**, printed **programme** but **have** their merchandise online.

The club have youth teams affiliated to the club in the form of Hadley Rangers who use the 3g pitch adjacent to the ground. It's a small sized pitch and also used for training for the 1st team.

Their main source of income is a real mixture - from the entrance admission, bar, hiring out the clubhouse, hiring the car park to the pub across the road, and of course 22 sponsors on board at different levels.

There is easy access to the ground from public transport - get on the Northern line(on the London tube), to the last stop which is High Barnet, then a 107 bus across the road which will take you 2 miles up the road past Arkley and get off at The Gate pub. Right opposite is Brickfield Lane, hence the nickname the Bricks. No signs here but just walk up the lane and there you have the ground and the Pavillion where you get a warm and friendly reception.

The history of the club is such that the club, formed in 1882, and have been at their present ground since 1922. In the early years they defeated that little known Middx side Spurs when they attracted crowds of several hundred to

Hadley Common. Jumping ahead to 2008, they ground shared with Potters Bar Town. Joining the Spartan South Midland League Division 2 and winning back to back promotions to reach step 5 by 2010/11.

Following £500k worth of facilities improvements, they came back to their present ground. 2019 - they joined the Essex Senior League for 2 seasons then came the FA restructuring. They finished 3rd in their league, but due to ground grading, the 2nd placed team - Risborough Rangers - were denied promotion. Under the PPG system, the club were handed promotion to their current level.

One player to look out for, amongst the many talented and skilful players in this vibrant team, is Isaac Stones who is on the radar of a number of step 3 clubs and above who are interested. He has already scored 12 goals in 12 games this season. The teams came out with Hadley in red tops(and white trim), black shorts, with Aylesbury in amber tops with Pirelli tyre marks over the front and back! The game itself was won in the second half by a solitary goal, in a closely fought game, 1-0 scored by the home teams defender Hermes Gbio. A disputed offside 'goal' from Aylesbury, and a stonewall penalty not given to Hadley kind of evened itself out.

This is definitely a club to go back to and not just a recommendation. You won't be disappointed.

HARBOUROUGH TOWN V BURY

FA CUP 4TH QUALIFYING ROUND

12/10/24

Welcome to the club from Market Harborough, a boom town from Leicestershire.

A club with 1,100 kids involved at youth level, a vets side, walk in football, a women's team, and of course the men's first team. With a vibrant youth section, they invariably have a pathway to the first team, from U12 to U23's.

They have 9 grass pitches, on a lease all taken off the councils hands, a clubhouse, two function rooms, 150 coaches at the club and are an FA 3 star accredited club.

The club is run as a business, as opposed to a traditional football club, a different way of running a football club for a new era.

They literally operate 7 days a week and have crowds of 400, which is increasing all the time. Alongside that they have 10 voluntary match day stewards, who provide a high quality service because of those experienced people they hire. Part of their job is looking after people with disabilities and also the match officials.

In speaking with CEO, Laurence Jones, who incidentally is also head of the National league at the FA, working also out of Wembley Stadium. He has had a 20 year career in refereeing, has worked with AFC Bournemouth, and is also director of Leicestershire and Rutland County FA. He informs me though that the club wasn't always as bright, and well run, as it is now.

The club have been at the ground since back in the late 90's, formed out of a merger between Harborough Imperial FC and Spencers FC, and in 2000 all the different clubs came together to create a proper clubhouse and pitch(artificial). In 2009 the new pitch was laid, however 2 years on and the club had run into financial difficulties. They were playing in the United Counties League and had 40 plus teams with 40 plus different bank accounts(all coming under the club name). Something had to be done about this, and in 2014 they had a vision to get the club forward to step 3(when they were in step 6!).

The need was to become self sustaining, to generate funding and raising own funds. The club created a four sided ground which literally transformed the club, and now they own 2 x 3g pitches outright. It does help working well with the local council but their structure as a club, so I'm informed, is complicated.

Like a business, they are spreading their risk - they have established 3 companies.

1. Harborough Town Community Trust. A charity which protects the ground for the future.

2. Harborough Town football Club Ltd. Ensuring you can pay players under this limited company which you can't do as a charity.

3. Harborough Town Trading. The profits are split between the first two.

You'll be pleased to know that the club regularly produce a programme and have a club shop.

As for expansion plans, under ground grading they are going to produce a new 100 seater stand, a 3rd turnstile, and an extra toilet. Also, and here they don't have to, but are erecting a new boardroom, a catering complex, a third 3g pitch, and an education building for the future.

The club are very ambitious and are looking to get into the National League, via a sustainability route.

They now have a chance to go even further than ever before, in the FA cup if they beat ex league opposition in Bury(who are incidentally a few steps/divisions below them in the pyramid).

This really is a club going places and one to look out for.

HENDON FC V WALTON & HERSHAM
SOUTHERN LEAGUE PREMIER DIVISION SOUTH

06/04/24

A short trip across town today to North West London and the home of Hendon FC.

Today's Southern League Premier South fixture, against Walton & Hersham, (NW London v Surrey) is also an annual tribute to one of their most famous, and most liked, players Dermot Drummy. I had the privilege of playing in the same school team, and classmates for 5 years, at our old school, Brooke House, in Clapton, London E5. Drummy went on to play for (naturally) Hackney schools - in the mid 70's Hackney schools being the 2nd best schools team in the whole of England only losing narrowly to the whole of Manchester schools in the schoolboys finals. A team that also included Mark Falco (ex Spurs & Rangers). He also played for Arsenal youth and reserve's(never quite made the first team), Blackpool, Hendon, Wealdstone, Enfield, St Albans, player manager at Ware, then managed Arsenal youth, Chelsea youth & U21's, a spell coaching in Japan, then manager of Crawley Town for 2 seasons.....until his untimely death in 2017.

Having spoken to two of his former colleagues - Erskine Smart, and Colin Tate, who produced some funny anecdotes regards Dermot, who was a real joker and quick witted with it. Dermot, in midfield, would often say to Erskine to "give me the ball and you'll do the running". He could just change a game that easily with his passing. A real quality player. At his funeral it was like a real who's who in football with the likes of Brendan Rogers, Liam Brady, Arsene Wenger, turning up to pay their respects.

Hendon, as a club, are 100% fan owned, have two main directors including Chairman Cyrus Cooper whom I got the run down on the club.

The ground, at Silver Jubilee Park, has a 3G pitch and the main seated stand leads back to the boardroom and further down the clubhouse and bar. Behind one goal is seated and covered and also has a private park bench! The opposite end is also covered but terraced. Opposite the main stand you have two terraced (and covered) areas on either side of the dug outs. The food facilities consist of a burger bar outside the clubhouse. There is also a disabled ramp from the clubhouse to the seats and terracing. The club shop, near the entrance, is well stocked with scarfs, hats, books, mugs, retro shirts. All in the home green colours, but no half and half of anything. This is non league not the Premiership. Proper football!

Manning the bar early at the ground, as well as claiming to do everything at the club, is none other than former Arsenal player Ian Allinson. His son is also the manager, and Jo, the Chairman's wife works in hospitality. A real family club.

Running with the current media trend going forward, the club currently have 14,000 followers on you tube, even though their average crowd is around 300. The capacity here is 1,990 but highest attendance here was 947 - a friendly v Arsenal in 2021.

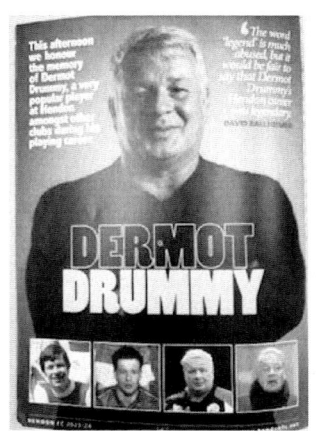

Onto the game and Walton get a penalty after 39 mins. The No.7 fluffs it and we go into HT at 0-0. It's a real windy and cold day, and the weatherman must have been on drugs when stated it was going to be 22• and summer. Really, it was warmer at Tow Law Town last week! Early into the 2nd half and Walton go 1-0 up. Hendon attack with a great move which hit the post. Then, soon after a good reflex save by the Hendon keeper - Dylan Berry - prevented a 2nd Walton goal. In the last minute a penalty gets awarded to Hendon. Up steps Joe White to blast into the low far corner to make it 1-1. The 8 mins added time made it more of an exciting finish but both teams shared the points in this score draw, in front of a crowd of 239.

This season the club amazingly knocked out former league club Oldham, on their own patch, before losing to Wealdstone in the next round of the FA trophy. However, the Greens have a great Amateur history. The club were formed in 1908 - began as Christchurch Hampstead. 1909/10 they were renamed Hampstead Town, then in 1926 just Hampstead. 7 years later changing to Golders Green.

Then in 1946 to their present name of Hendon. There was a previous club that reached the Q/F of the FA cup in 1883. In 1932, the old Hendon club met Hampstead to raise funds for that old Hendon club. In 1963, they entered the Isthmian League where they stayed until 2018. They won the FA Amateur cup 3 times in 1960, 1965, 1972, and the final of 1955 v Bishop Auckland, drew a crowd of over 100,000. They also took Newcastle Utd to a draw in the FA cup 3rd round of 1974.

In the 1950's Hendon were the first club to win a floodlight cup match, when they beat Arsenal in the London Challenge cup at Highbury. They have also won their last 3 visits to Highbury. Their original colours were blue, and after wearing green for a long period, they changed back to blue in 1997/98...and then 2 years later back to green!

The main problem at their home ground is that there are no signs anywhere, along the way, or even immediately outside the ground, notifying you of the club playing there. Although this is a private ground, there are restrictions outside from the local council, due to pressure from local householders who obviously don't like the football club being there. Cyrus Cooper, new chairman of 1 season, has been a supporter of the club since age 7, watching Hendon play at their old Claremont Road ground since 1972. They were made to leave that ground in 2008 when their main sponsor - Arbiter Group - wanted to sell up. They subsequently ground shared at Wembley FC, and Harrow Borough, until they met Rob Morris of KTMC investors who offered the club the premises to play on, rent free on a 10 year lease. The ground is jointly owned by Rob Morris & Dan Manzi.

Currently in the Southern League they need to get back to the Isthmian league as their travelling costs are crippling the club due to the high petrol/coach costs. Every year they appeal to leave the Southern League. Every year the FA reject their appeal.

Players to look out for are the younger players Sam Adenola and Joe White, along with the more established of Billy Leonard & Niko Muir-Merchant.

HERNE BAY V NORTHWOOD
FA CUP 2ND QUALIFYING ROUND

07/09/24

A 55 minute drive to the North Kent coast, to get a real in depth feel for this community interest company of Herne Bay FC. A club that's run with the enthusiasm and relentless drive of Chairman Matt Barman backed up with long standing stalwart John Bathurst. The club with a real community feel and a passion for its local people, combined with charitable work, makes it a solid community club.

Today they face Northwood, in the FA Trophy 1st qualifying round, with the club currently undefeated in league and cup games. The club have recently revamped their ground with a new clubhouse, which is a real community hub open every morning for the local community. Along the main walkway from near the turnstile to the clubhouse, that side has been freshly tarmacked. The 3G pitch was laid at the start of the 2022/23 season, when promoted to the Isthmian Premier league, and the club ground shared with Ramsgate whilst the pitch was being laid, financed partly by the Football Foundation/Valencia community fund/four main investors, and various grants. Incidentally Velocity were the company that built the pitch.

The committee room(ex radio room)is to be changed into the match day sponsorship and hospitality to include a bar and a cafe. Other alterations will be to erect PV panels onto the main stand, to generate electricity and cut down on the bills. There will also be EV charging points. Other plans are to build a new soft play area at the back of the clubhouse, and on the other side of the ground a caged football net for youngsters and where teams can also warm up. Then after the game the youngsters can use it rather than running onto the pitch at the end!

The old stand, opposite the clubhouse, was built in 1955. It will be retained but the asbestos roof will be replaced and likewise the old red seats(formerly from the local pier), with new blue seats added akin to club colours.

There is a great tie up with 'Strode park foundation'. A charitable work in helping the local community. The new chairman, Matt who was formerly manager at Kent side Lordswood, describes his vision and how his inspiration is to promote a real attractive brand of football within. The 5 year aim is to focus on getting 5 players from the youth team into the first team. To make, and sustain, a model in which to promote more opportunities for the youth section. They currently have teams ranging from U13 to U23's, with Herne Bay Harriers having 21 youth teams to come over to the club.

Their aim at the club is to 'be the best'(not necessarily the biggest)and that youth plan, over 3-5 years, is just starting and heavily focussed on the match day experience. Money is being pumped back into the clubhouse for improvements, plus also into the youth section. The current manager, Steve Lovell(ex Gillingham and a Welsh international)has retained all his players that he wanted to keep here when he arrived. The youth team, up to U16, get free admission to all league games and there is a resident DJ who plays here before and after the game.

A typical match day Saturday would be - 8am cafe open for breakfast. 12-3pm DJ, match, then DJ and in the evening everyone allowed in for free with entertainment, and the clubhouse is also used for other events. This gives you a real social/community feel for the whole day and night. Their aim is to get an increase of at least 100 in the crowd every season, making the club sustainable season by season. They have 3 veterans teams and they keep ex players as part of their club. The volunteers are an important part of the club, of which some are there at least a few days a week from 8am to 10 pm, creating the Herne Bay family - to support local residents.

They recently entertained a Spurs 'Legends' side against the club vets. This resulted in a massive crowd, for their standards of 4,000, over twice their alleged capacity! For next season the FA are going to make all clubs, at this level, assess their capacity. One of the ex Spurs players now wants to use the facilities, and the spin off from the large crowd was gaining new season ticket holders and awareness of the club. Some of the money made, after expenditure, went to various charities. A worthy club indeed. The Bay now face Hendon in the next round after their 1-0 victory today.

HERTFORD TOWN V HENDON TOWN
SOUTHERN LEAGUE DIVISION 1 CENTRAL
23/07/24

Over to the scenic countryside of Hertfordshire and home to Hertford Town of the Southern League Division 1 Central (step 4). Tonight taking on Hendon (step 3) in another warm July friendly fixture.

Meeting Chairman Colin Hay in the boardroom I get the lowdown on the club over coffee by Shelagh, and also attended by director of football Graham Oakeby.

Hertford Town were originally founded in 1908 and have been at their current ground since the late 1950's - a real old school ground but gradually being added to including the 3 year old 3g pitch. Adding this pitch was a godsend as, like a few clubs, the pitch was heavily flooded over the years and lies on a floodplain. There is only one narrow road in to the ground over a small bridge, but plenty of car parking outside the ground and around to the side which they've recently opened up. The main stand looks like the original stand, yet with added plastic tip up seats. Behind one goal is a full length covered terrace walkway whereas the opposite end, and opposite the main stand, are just open walkways.

Their expansion plans are - phase 1 already happened with the 3g pitch, new car park, and new showers. The old pumps for the showers were antiquated as they were there since the '50's and were originally used for the two large baths that clubs originally had! Phase 2 will be the new clubhouse and bar to replace existing, and phase 3 to replace the boardroom with new.

Colin came in appx 5 years ago, along with Marc Sinfield, both as assistant managers. Ben Heard also came in around that time and is the player manager and director of the club. Ben also runs the BHPP Academy and they play in the U19 National League. He was previously a player at the likes of Watford, Shrewsbury, Oxford United, Boreham Wood, St Albans, and Hemel Hempstead. When these guys came in, the club was completely run down financially and would have gone under if they hadn't saved them. A lot of debtors came out of 'the wood work' which they weren't aware of and had to be settled first. A good introduction to the club for them! Now they are on a healthy keel.

Colin informs me that Ben's academy is the way forward especially when they have 500 youngsters affiliated to the club with over 30 youth - boys and girls - and also ladies, walk in football, and an all inclusive team which they lay on mini tournaments for as well. The academy they have will also be branching out to a girls section shortly and they have, as a club, achieved a 3 star accreditation from the FA. At a club of this size, it's mind blowing the amount of background work and admin they have to go through at all levels. The capacity at the ground is 2,500 with an average of around 300. Although the stadium is surrounded by trees with very peaceful surroundings, it's only a 5 minute walk away from the centre of town. A club on the up and a ground well worth checking out before the development starts, especially when they play local rivals Ware! Tonight's game was a tough test for Hertford, in their familiar blue and white, as Hendon are a very strong physical side and didn't let up with their challenges. Hendon went 1-0 up in the first half, in their all orange ish fluorescent strip, and finished 4-0 winners.

ILKESTON TOWN V BASFORD UNITED
NORTHERN PREMIER LEAGUE PREMIER DIVISION
20/01/24

One of the few games on, and yes it is a marvellous 4G pitch, and over to Ilkeston Town v Basford United - a local derby game and Derbyshire v Nottinghamshire. 12th v 18th in this Northern Premier League Premier Division. I Arrived here via a brief stop at Matlock Town to find their game off with a frozen pitch!

The stadium is unique in that it has a clock tower, which is situated where one of the corner flags are. It houses the boardroom above and dressing rooms below. Alongside at the top is a small seated stand mostly for media and officials. Further down, on the same side are two more seated stands lower down but interrupted by home and away seated areas. They are definitely not dug outs and blend into the seated stands, but gated off from the public at both ends.

Behind one goal is covered terracing and the opposite end is uncovered. The other side of the pitch is a walkway and also houses a large bar and clubhouse, a sponsors/members lounge, and a food bar. Not forgetting the club shop, located at the uncovered end and built like a small conservatory.

….3 mins gone and Ilkeston (playing in the old familiar Ajax strip of red and white) go 1-0 up with a goal from no.11 Jamie Walker. I was told to look out for him before the game! Then on 20 mins keeper Matthew Yates dived down, to clasp the ball, and prevent a certain goal for Basford from a downward header, and it's 2-0 now with a brace from Mr Walker, and on 38 mins the home side are 3-0 up curtesy of no.4 Declan Errat-Thompson.

In the boardroom at HT, the directors of Basford Utd just look plain bemused!

The hospitality was very cordial and great chatting to one of the volunteers who is an Ayr United fan. Unusual but he's emigrated down South and likes it here!

More of the same in the second half with Ilkeston scoring but disallowed for offside. Later on Jamie Walker finishes off a great team passing movement for the teams 4th goal and his hat trick. Basford pull a goal back a couple of mins before the end of normal time to make it a 4-1 final score to Ilkeston, with unsurprisingly Jamie Walker voted MOTM. The second half watched from the warmth of the indoor clock tower!

In speaking with secretary Mark Frost, the club has excellent facilities which attracts good footballers from elsewhere. They have a fantastic ladies team, run by Kelly who also doubles up working behind the bar on match days!

The club has over 400 junior members and are really community driven in recruiting fans and players alike.

The club is in the DE7 postcode of Derbyshire, but just next to the border with Nottinghamshire. The river, behind the bar/clubhouse side of the ground, separates the two counties. In fact the original contour of the river went directly through where the pitch is today. This was before the new ground was built, and which the river was then physically moved back to accommodate the new ground! This was 33 years ago and on only one occasion has a game been postponed due to flooding, not the ground itself mind you but the main road flooded and no cars could get in/out of the ground!

The new pitch was due to be laid in May 2021. Their Derbyshire neighbours, Mickleover FC, were due to have theirs laid in March 2021. When the Mickleover pitch was laid, someone broke into that clubs ground, with a digging truck, and lifted the whole pitch up and stole off into the night! Unbelievable. No idea if they were ever caught. Anyway, because of that the company who were due to lay the pitch for Ilkeston, went back as an emergency and re laid another pitch for Mickleover. Ilkeston then got another company in - Polytan - who were looking at installing a pitch at St George's Park. Polytan offered to install the new 4g pitch at Ilkeston to showcase their work. This is the company who are the producers of the finest pitches in the country so it all worked out well for the club. At the same time they had a sprinkler system installed all the way around the pitch, and on a timer as well. Since then Marine FC have also had installed the same high quality pitch

They have also recently installed new lights to their floodlights which were very outdated.

A club definitely going places.

KNAPHILL V AFC CROYDON ATHLETIC
COMBINED COUNTIES PREMIER DIVISION SOUTH PLAY OFF FINAL

07/05/24

It's the Combined Counties Premier Division South final tonight - Knaphill FC v AFC Croydon Athletic.

What a difference a day makes with beautiful warm sunshine in the countryside of Surrey, not far from Woking, to see a really well organised, and hospitable, club on the way up.

Knaphill are now in their centenary year and not only on the verge of going up into the Isthmian League but having a centenary shirt designed with a mix of different kits over the years all rolled into one! It's now half white half reddish, similar to Wokings kit, and as sported by current fixture secretary Nick Croshaw. Getting here early I spoke to Chairman Chris Drane, who was acting in the capacity of kitman at the time! Chris informs me that the budget for this season was intended to get them promotion this season. They have been nothing but consistent this season being in 2nd place for the majority of the season. They have a great young keeper in Josh Barker who has represented England Uni's and has been approached by club's higher up the leagues to the National League, but he's here with the club he loves for the foreseeable future.

The ground is council owned and at present has only a licence to play on it, not even on a lease...yet. It is indeed a Beautiful Ground, and as such should feature prominently in this book 2. It's surrounded by trees and countryside and looks glorious in tonight's sunshine. It has 2 x 50 seater covered identikit stands. One behind the goal with black seats, the other along the length of the pitch, opposite the dug outs, with black and red seats - the team colours. The facilities are within in the clubhouse with bar and kitchen next to each other. The bar doubles up as club shop which I've seen at a few grounds. Lisa Fance doing a great job in the small boardroom which accommodates away directors as well. Her father, Dave Holloway, was also manager of the club back in 1979/80 so a real family connection.

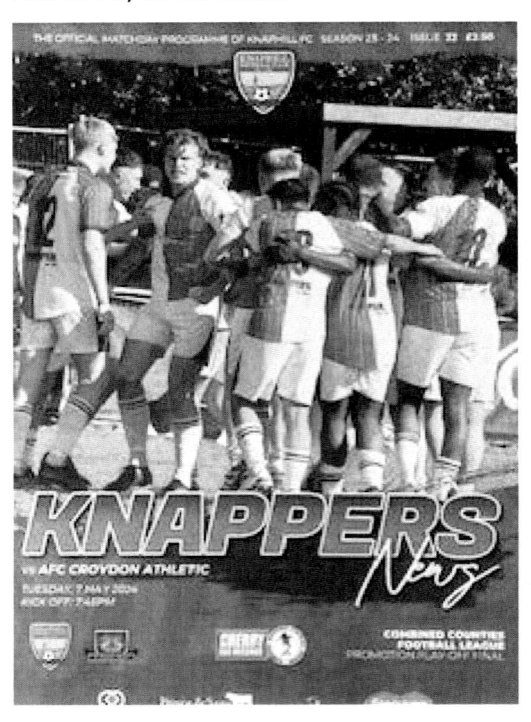

Kick off delayed to 8pm now due to the large crowds. It's going to be a record breaking crowd tonight breaking Saturdays record of 570. They've actually shut the turnstiles after 750 in, probably on police advice! The club have even opened up the far goal end, which was previously closed off, to accommodate the crowd coming in.

18 mins in and a bit of a cagey game at present…..even Stormzy has made an appearance now!...44 mins and Croydon go 1-0 up. A few minutes into the second half and Croydon get a 2nd with a breakaway goal. With the Knaphill keeper keeping them in the game, it's now game on with a penalty for the home side. He then skies it well over the bar and then in the ensuing melee,

for whatever reason, he gets sent off and the ref dishes out a couple of yellow cards as well. It's now 10 v 11 and still 0-2. Now another pen to the home, and this time emphatically put away. Now 1-2 and the Croydon keeper gets booked for holding onto the ball. An enthralling finish to the game with the score at 1-2 and AFC Croydon follow Farnham Town in getting promotion from this division.

Incidentally, the club have been going 1924 starting off in the Surrey Intermediate League. However, by the 1970's the club were playing in the Woking & District league.

The club have come leaps and bounds from County football to now being established as top side in step 5 and looking for promotion this season to step 4 and ultimately the Isthmian South Central. Do check out the club, facilities, and scenary.

LEAMINGTON V AFC SUDBURY
SOUTHERN LEAGUE PREMIER CENTRAL DIVISION

27/04/24

Over to Warwickshire for the last Saturday league game of the season. It's the home of the 'Brakes' of Leamington FC v the boys from Suffolk - AFC Sudbury.

All to play for as the home team need to win for a home tie in the play off semi final, and the away team need to win/draw to stay up. A great friendly club on the up, when they move into their new stadium in town in 4 years time! A good attendance here of 847 with the average attendance being around the 550 mark. Last season Leamington were relegated from the National League North and Sudbury were promoted from the Isthmian North. That could be reversed again today.

The ground here in the countryside has a two covered seated stand opposite each other, one with a burger bar to one side, and the dug outs, and the other side with the club shop which opened upon request. The covered terrace end is also where the players come out, and houses the clubhouse, boardroom and meeting room. In speaking with one of the directors - Kevin Watson - The club have been at this ground since 2000 and are looking to move away to a new ground centrally in town. When this comes to fruition it will be a real community hub. A small village in itself with an athletics ground, new housing, technology plant, retail, BMW car plant, and landscaped. The lay out will also encourage people to walk to the ground. The club will sell the current ground to the council and be playing on the new council owned ground, on a 150 year lease, and at a 'peppercorn' rent. They will also be able to generate more income from all areas - facilities, hiring pitch. The capacity there will be 5,000 and can be extended if they were to get to the EFL. The club have been in discussion with the local authority for the past 10 years. When this eventually happens, this will totally transform the the football club (and community)which will make it far more sustainable.

Going back to 1987 though, and it was a club in decline. The ground was sold off by the owners, a factory, (not club owners) and therefore had nowhere to go. In fact they were without a playing club for 13 years. At that time they were known as AP Leamington. In between time they were fund raising over those years and had to start again in the Midland Combined Division 2 (step 7). A massive difference now with a well run club and a board of 6 directors steering the club in the right direction.

As for the game - it was 0-0 at HT. Leamington creating the chances but not getting very far. As the Stranglers would say, Something better change (for the 2nd half), and indeed it did with the home side getting the better of Sudbury by 2 goals, scored in the first few minutes of the half, and the second the latter part, by Callum Stewart & Jack Edwards, the numbers 9 & 10 respectively. This didn't stop the yellow army of dressed up Sudbury fans who sang throughout the whole game and created a great atmosphere - nice to see Ali G, Jesus, a priest, blues brother, tellytubby, Snow White, a bottle of beer, and a nun all singing together!

Tracing the club back to its original roots and you go back to 1933, when it was Lockheed, Borg & Beck- a car parts company. In 1947 the company bought the Windmill ground from Coventry City, who had themselves bought the ground in 1937 for their 'A' team after Leamington Town had folded. It was not until the 1970's that the current colours of gold and black came about when someone made an error when ordering the new kit! 1973 - Lockheed became Autmotive Products and the club became AP Leamington as the club are more widely remembered. In 1983, Leamington FC were formed with the intention of buying the Windmill ground. The association with AP ended in July 1985 and the club reverted to Leamington FC. Come 1990, a field was purchased from a local farmer and levelled. Re launched in 2000, the club did not look back.

The club claim to have the best highlights package in non league football on you tube, so do check it out. It started off with a couple of students, from Warwickshire Uni wanting to create a film for their media studies. They've now kept those guys on as a permanent role. Two past players of mention are - Colby Bishop, a striker who went to Accrington Stanley to become their top goal scorer, then onto Portsmouth to be their top striker. Josh March who went on to play for Forest Green Rovers.

The current manager - Paul Holleran - has been manager now since 2007 and over 700 games. He's overseen 2 promotions and has done really well on the clubs small budget. He also attracts good local young players to the club. Apart from the two goal scorers today Stewart (a player from the youth team) and Edwards, there is also Callum Hawkins, a goalkeeper previously with Burton Albion, and player of the season, at right back, Dan Meredith.

The club has a Brakes Community Foundation Trust - aside from being a charitable trust it helps run a co op supporters club, which runs a mini bus service to, and from, town for the supporters on the day of the game.There is also a Vice Presidents club - marked for fundraising. They also have a meeting room which the chamber of commerce use to promote the club and get sponsors.

This club, once moved into the new community stadium, can really take off in a big way and pushing for league status eventually.

MICKLEOVER V AFC TELFORD UNITED
SOUTHERN LEAGUE PREMIER CENTRAL
06/01/24

Its over to Derbyshire today for this top of the table clash with both teams in good form.

A real pleasant surprise of a ground looking superb and well kept. The glorious sunshine made the 3G pitch look even better.

The bar in the clubhouse is getting packed as time goes on today and there is another bar tucked away at another entrance I found.

The main hospitality suite is further down the pitch and there is a great view of the game from the platform above.

A club well run by a great character and businessman in Don Amott. A former director at Derby County and Derby born & bred. He runs a successful motor homes business, and he actually played at a decent level himself. Previously owned 30% of Derby County with a consortium including Mel Morris but went into administration.

Don was approached by Mickleover to take the club forward which he has done in no uncertain terms, giving the club a new lease of life. The club are a CIC - Community Interest Club.

Like all clubs though at this level its most run by volunteers, with the likes of

Charles Harrison in the hospitality suite/sponsors/directors, Neil the car park attendant, Charlie Divers on security/safety, and secretary Darren McKay(whom I originally met at an away game v Kettering).

Chris Head, the architect, it was who designed and developed the ground with a £150K grant on top of the £750K cost paid. This was taken out on an 8 year loan which the club pays back. They self generate income through sponsors far more than most other clubs and hold a concert, with 4,000 attending, in August with fireworks.

The club have been at their present ground since 1993 and were established as Mickleover Sports in 1948, shortening their name to Mickleover FC in 2020. Their previous ground was at Vicarage Park, 1 mile from the present ground, and Paul Duffin, former 1st team and reserves in the late 80's, was involved in the move.

Tony Shaw was at the club since 1993 as manager(as well as a PE teacher at the same time), and Secretary until 2 years ago(1994-2021). Nowadays the club has recruited in their ranks 5/6 ex professional players from the likes of Burton Albion and Sheffield Wednesday. Their manager - John McGrath - has been manager for the past 7 years(the club keep their staff and stay loyal to them)

and the proof is in the pudding with the recent success of Mickleover in their highest position ever.

Celebrities abound around the stadium with boards surrounding the pitch shining a light on the England 66 players, Brian Clough, and even Cricketing celebrities - Don Amott was previously Chairman at Derbyshire County cricket club. A previous player Matt Oakley went to Exeter City when Steve Perryman was running them. Friendships have developed since and likewise with Ex Derby and Arsenal star Charlie George who makes an appearance at the club once/twice a season.

Derby County run the academy committee trust on the education side here, but they pay rent to Mickleover - sounds like good business to me!

The crowds have gradually increased over the years to an average of now 400, in fact they've doubled over the last few years.

Players to look out for are Finn Delap(son of Rory) and Ethan Mann at age 19 both centre backs. Despite the 1-0 loss today the club are still very much in play off contention and I would highly recommend anyone to check this club out.

MILDENHALL TOWN V WROXHAM
ISTHMIAN LEAGUE NORTH

05/10/24

A glorious sunny day here in Suffolk for another Isthmian North Division game, this time between Mildenhall Town and the northerners from Norfolk, Wroxham. A well run club with 10 good people, paid bar staff and groundsman, with a perfect grass pitch. Speaking to the Chairman - Bill Flynn, a real character, Jon Sadler the general manager and accountant, and Ryan Townsin the vice chairman, who all give me the run down on this friendly town club which is a real hub of the community. The club, originally founded in 1898, have been at their current ground since post WW2. The pitch is looking fantastic, the clubhouse is spacious with large tv screens, a hospitality suite, a main seated stand on that side with another covered stand. Opposite you have the Cameron Hotel (one of the clubs sponsors) seated stand. Behind both goals are at present huge conifer hedges. These will be going soon as the club plan to erect covered terraced stands behind the goals with fencing/brickwork to finish off.

The club have the RAF bases nearby with Mildenhall and Lakenheath. The Americans have their own base there and we're expecting a number of them to turn up today and be educated with proper football! This is a real 6 pointer today as both clubs, at this early stage, are in the wrong half of the table so concentrating on the league as they're out of the cups. Going back 3 years, the club decided to relieve the manager of his duties and after the game they met giving him his notice on the pitch,at the away game v Grantham. That sounds like a first! The last game of the season was still to be played and half the team had walked out upset that their manager had been sacked! A new manager came in quickly and found a number of players to complete their last game of the season. It obviously worked as last season they were Thurlow Nunn Eastern Counties champions by 14 points and only 15 goals against.

The clubs long standing goalkeeper, since age 17, is Josh Pope brother of Nick Pope at Newcastle. In a bizarre quirk of fate, both goalkeepers were sent off in the same week. Coincidence or what. Today Josh Pope puts on a terrific performance keeping Mildenhall in the game with 4 excellent saves. Another player that shone out was the right back, Ben Nolan, who gets forward and pulled one goal back for the home side. A classy player at this level.

The club hold an annual HALL FEST, held during the close season, where they have around 6/7 bands playing on the pitch which generates vital income for the club. They also hold a fireworks night, with a crowd of around 1500, and a family fun day in memory of long serving Martin Law, 30 years with the club, and an ex player, who died with MND.

The clubhouse was built in 1992 and hosts live music every Friday night, and as mentioned a real community hub and open 6 days a week. This build came from lottery funding, football improvement fund, and a bank loan. The pitch is council owned but all facilities are owned by the club. They are looking to expand with adding another hospitality suite as they have to have, at this level, a separate suite for the away directors and also one for sponsors.

The youth section has been successfully run by Trevor Bennett. They have pitches to play on locally at Barton Mills to, therefore grow youth football, with 4 teams and 3 new ones coming on board. There are also new pitches, built by the council next to the ground, to supply more youth teams, and for the 1st team to train on (although not a full size pitch). The 1st team currently train on the main pitch. The U16 academy jumps up to the U23's so a big step there.

The ground is named the Riverside stadium, who are one of the clubs biggest sponsors(Riverside hotel) run by venture group with Brian Keane. Bill, the Chairman, is very hands on and feels strongly about the club existing as a very important part of the town. He was originally vice chairman from 2002 before stepping up in 2018.

Great news is that they are planning a new club shop in the ground, as well as currently online and with a local sports shop. The club badge looks a real old fashioned style but is very simplistic and designed back in the 1980's, looking effective at the same time....and the slope on the pitch goes from the goalmouth to the end of the opposite corner flag down 1.1m!

Their objective is to stay up this season and with manager Phil Weavers at the helm (ex fireman and Bury Town!) they have every chance of doing so with an average attendance of 270.

NEWMARKET TOWN V WALTHAMSTOW
ISTHMIAN NORTH DIVISION

28/09/24

Over to Newmarket Town today, not for the races today though, but to see the football club play their first ever home league game at step 4 level. Welcome to the Isthmian League North Division here in Suffolk.

Newmarket were promoted last season, via the play offs, after having beaten Barton in the final. Today they play East London side Walthamstow.

A long standing club going back to 1877, and moving to their present ground where they have been for the past 139 years. Affectionately known as the 'Jockeys' and the Jockey club in town mainly sponsor the youth teams. Speaking of youth, all their team members(plus one adult)get free admission to all league games. There is also 10% off goods in Newmarket sports shop where they sell the club tops. Newmarket have a vibrant youth section with a pathway to the 1st team. This is clearly evident when you have 6 players currently in the 1st team squad from the youth team, including the likes of outstanding talent like Ryan Cole, recognised as the best prospect here in ages. A couple of other young talents have gone on to bigger clubs - Harry Darling to Swansea and also Tom Knowles. Not forgetting the girls teams run by Dom Szary, who is now club secretary, managing the teams to 6 league titles.

Both boys & girls teams start training from U6's and the Juniors are based in the EJA League which is of a very good standard. Their 3G pitch, built in 2016, and still going strong, was funded mostly by the club by selling land that they owned.

Like a lot of clubs, the pitch usage is high and is the main income, with Cambridge Utd development team, and also Kings Lynn U23's, who both train and play here respectively.

The club produce a good glossy programme and club merchandise is sold behind the bar. Capacity, I've been informed by vice chairman Colin Bithell, is around 3,000 with a record crowd of over 2,000 v Cambridge Utd in the 1940's. More recently they had over 1,000 versus the same club, arranged as a charity game, for two of their players who were disabled in a lorry incident. Their average crowd is around 200 and last season in the play off final(the first ever play off final in the Thurlow Nunn League)they had a crowd of just under a 1,000.

Other charitable work has gone on in the form of hosting charity tournaments in the summer, helping the local air ambulance, and cancer charity, and also donating to local food banks. Due to recent promotional success the ground grading requirements are - to erect new toilet, new car park, new committee room, and enlarge the away dressing rooms. The clubs plan is to grow the club organically through both the youth & ladies teams.

Manager, Michael Shinn, is the longest serving manager in local leagues, having achieved promotion with an existing squad initially only bringing in a few players. Only 2 of their players are on contracts, both of them younger players.

The ground itself has a main seated stand holding 144 seats, built in 1996 in the yellow & blue home colours. Alongside this are the dressing rooms, and clubhouse. Outside the clubhouse is a covered walkway leading to a covered small section of seats. Behind both goals are open walkways, with one end housing picnic benches, and a hospitality room, next to a medical room. There are great views from the main stand looking out to part of the racecourse, and on the opposite side are the dug outs, electronic scoreboard and digital clock.

Their main local rivals in this league are, Bury Town, Mildenhall, and Cambridge City. Todays game was won 4-1 by Walthamstow, who scored two early goals within 6 goals. It was more of a game of the opposition took their chances and the home side didn't. Closer than the scoreline suggests.

NORTH GREENFORD UNITED V ARDLEY UNITED
COMBINED COUNTIES LEAGUE PREMIER NORTH

12/08/23

Over to the North West part of London today to check out North Greenford United. Playing host to Ardley United in the Combined Counties League Premier Division North.

The all blues v the yellows and it's Middlesex v Oxfordshire.

The ground consists of a seated grandstand, behind one goal, alongside a covered terrace section where the noisier fans congregate! Then you have another covered terrace section to one side, and the rest is open walkways.

A great bunch of friendly geezers here with the likes of fervent fans like Chris Hewitt, and not withstanding the staff who do a brilliant job including running the bar.

The two clubs have been formed respectively in 1944 & 1945. A strange time to form a club during the war but that's what it states on the pin badge at Greenford that Richard Rooney (one of two vice chairman's) kindly presented to me at HT.

Volunteers at clubs like this are essential and nice to meet Paul Mills at HT - Paul is joint first team manager and chairman, and his wife runs the bar!....1-0 to Greenford at HT in a closely fought game...the noise goes up a notch as they nearly get a second...and then the final score stays at 1-0 to the home side and could easily have been more.

The history of the club goes back to 1944 when they were first formed as a youth team. The following season saw the formation of a senior side with the club entering the Harrow League and later the Middlesex County League.

In 1983 the club was promoted to the spartan league, but in 1994 resigned to re-join the Middlesex League. In 2002 ground improvements were undertaken, including floodlights, to join the Combined Counties League.

In 2003/04, they reached the final of the Premier Challenge cup losing to AFC Wimbledon in front of over 5000 at Woking FC. The following year they finished runners up in the League. In 2006/07, under Mick Harvey they lost to Merstham in the League cup final. That following season they finished runners up in the League under new manager Steve Ringrose The 2009/10 season proved to be the most successful in the clubs history when they became League champions and promoted to the Southern League Division 1 Central, also winning the MFA charity cup beating Enfield Town 1-0 at Hampton & Richmonds ground.

Over the next few seasons a period of struggle ensued till relegation took hold in 2015/16. In 2018/19, the club were moved to the Spartan South Midlands League. They survived that season and are now on the up after finishing this season with a great cup run in the FA Vase competition.

PETEROROUGH SPORTS V DARLINGTON
NATIONAL LEAGUE NORTH

07/11/23

National League North fixture up in Cambridgeshire tonight - Peterborough Sports v Darlington.

Another up and coming club who are trying to establish themselves in this division(2nd season here), but taken over at the helm is new owner Tim Woodward who has a plan of taking them up to the National League in 2/3 seasons. Currently though this is more of a bottom half clash but with Peterborough on a 5 game unbeaten run. Darlo have bought down a number of their faithful fans including Glen, well into his 80's now, who runs the club travel!

First blood to the Turbines of Peterborough are 1-0 up through Ocean Gallagher. Now 2-0 after 55 mins. Final score of 2-0 despite the continuous attacking play from the away team.

The club were originally founded in 1908 with the name Brotherhoods engineering works. In 1990's the club were named Bearings direct (sounds like an online Stock Exchange team!)

123

The ground has undergone a major revamp since 2012, funded by the social club, football foundation and the former manager/chairman.

They once played Spurs (that small Middlesex team) at Lincoln Road, before WW2, in front of a 4,000 crowd.

Their most famous player is Vic Watson, who played in the Northants League title winning team of 1919/20, before signing for West Ham for the princely sun of £50! Vic Watson still remains West Ham's record scorer to this day.

A club with a great set of volunteers, from a steward who gets on well with all home and away fans, fantastic bar staff, cooks, turnstile operators, secretary Jonathan Robinson. They do a very tasty hot cheese & tomato slice for £2.50 at one side of the bar, and on other side they sell scarfs, mugs etc.

Capacity is currently 3,000. They recently changed their colours from blue & yellow to orange & black, though not popular with everyone, all the fans and volunteers back the chairman with all the good work he's doing for the club.

After tonight the club have now gone 6 games unbeaten and climbing up the league!

RAMSGATE V CHICHESTER CITY
ISTHMIAN SOUTH EAST DIVISION PLAY OFF SEMI FINAL

30/04/24

Back to the Isle of Thanet, to the club with the biggest youth section of teams in the whole of the county of Kent with 76.

Ramsgate are odds on favourites being 20 points ahead of Chi City in this division, but it doesn't always work out like that as we know.

Average crowds for this club are around the 1,500 mark and easily the best supported team in the area. The club usually let in all U18's free of charge + 1 adult free as well. The spend with the big crowds soon adds up with all food & drink bought.

The club has plans afoot to develop their ground further with grants from the Football Foundation, Sport England, and anyone else who'll give them the money for the new £3M stand to be built on the side of the present car park. This will incorporate not only the new covered seated stand but also hospitality, work units for the club, and the youth academy. Definitely a club on the up, let alone promotion to the Isthmian Premier when that happens. Their youth section has been proven with 4/5 local lads in the first team already. Still a good crowd here tonight of 1,462 despite the heavy coastal rain. Players to look out for are - Tom Hadler the goalkeeper(ex Maidstone), Joe Taylor the leading goal scorer, the twin brothers Alfie Paxman & Jack A Paxman, and ex Man Utd player Lee Martin. The 3G pitch is practically used 7 days a week, therefore all youngsters getting a chance to showcase their skills.

The expansion plans are obviously promotion, but the infrastructure will see a new £3M stand with hospitality and work units for the club/academy, being built at the start of this 2024/25 season as a 2-3 year plan. The clubs main sponsors are local builders WW Martin and the board of 8 directors is elected every 3 years.

The club also have a song, played at all home games, titled 'Ramsgate are massive' - recorded in time for the FA cup game v AFC Wimbledon his season just finished.

The ground itself has a covered seated main stand - Colin Hill stand - alongside the bar/directors room/corner flag bar. Behind both goals are covered terracing, real old school style, and at the far end goal there are 'Panna' football cages for the kids to play in, which is quite unique. The hot food favourite is the Ramsburger!

Improvements have been made over the past couple of seasons with the addition of the new bar with posts cemented in hoisting up awnings to protect on wet & hot days. The clubhouse is situated outside the ground.

James Lawson is the dynamic Chairman taking the club up to a higher level in so many ways and you cant help being impressed with the number of youth teams at the club and the number of children attending home games. The club have had over 500 children regularly attending the clubs Holiday Activity and Food(HAF)programmes and have provided a unique opportunity to for them to offer education and employment options to families, and in partnership with the digital poverty scheme, they were able to issue 400 laptops to the families. During the year 50 children were taught to swim and 40 children to ride their bikes. 150 children were taken on helicopter flights during their summer programme!

The average crowd has risen from 170 in 2021/22 to 1075 in 2023/24 - a massive increase. The away travel is subsidised at £10 per person to enable families to enjoy football away days and 20,000 hot meals have been prepared for children on all their programmes previously mentioned.

The history - it seems that the club have been at their ground since like forever! Although they have changed the position of the pitch around. Lets go back to 1886 for the earliest reincarnation of Ramsgate FC, but folded in 1924, with local rivals Ramsgate Glenville taking over their Southwood Stadium. Glenville did not reform after WW2 and a new club - Ramsgate Athletic - took over. The club actually retained the Athletic name until 1972. They played in the original incarnation of the Kent League until the League collapsed in 1959.

They then went on to the Southern League, did well but were to resign and drop down to the reformed Kent league in 1976. Jumping ahead to 2004 former manager Jim Ward led the club to two consecutive championships - Kent League Premier Division & Isthmian League 1st Division, then further taking the club into the Isthmian Premier Division, reaching the semi finals of the play offs in their 2nd season and winning the Isthmian League cup. Last season they reached the FA Cup 2nd round for the first time ever beating Cray Wanderers, and Woking along the way before losing to AFC Wimbledon.

The game itself was played in torrential rain at times and surprised it was actually completed. On 36 mins Billy Bioletti shoots over the bar and the rain lashing down turned into hailstones! 44 mins and a tap into an empty net and the lino flags for offside. So, still 0-0 at HT and the second half continued with the constant Ramsgate pressure......but its Chichester who score on 86 mins with a breakaway goal totally against the run of play. The ref adds on an additional 8 mins, so the players can get soaked even more! On 94 mins Chi City hit the post with a long range lob. Into the 100th minute(looks like extra additional time being played here), and a few more corners but not enough to get that equaliser and Chi go onto the final.

RAYNERS LANE REVIEW
SOUTHERN LEAGUE CENTRAL PREMIER DIVISION

23/09/24

A newly promoted London club that are now up to step 4 after success in the play offs from the Combined Counties League.

They, along with Cockfosters and Arsenal, are the North London teams with tube lines named after the team. Other North London teams take note!

The team were originally founded in 1933 and named after a local farmer, Daniel Rayner, and have been at the same ground since inception. He wouldn't recognise the ground now as it is a real local community hub, with part of the surrounding wasteland sold to developers with the deal being that the developers would build a new clubhouse and 3g pitch as well as building lots(and there are lots!)of townhouses adjacent to the ground. This arrangement has worked out well for both parties and the club have now a great solid base, ground and clubhouse going forward which they would never have had the opportunity to have had previously.

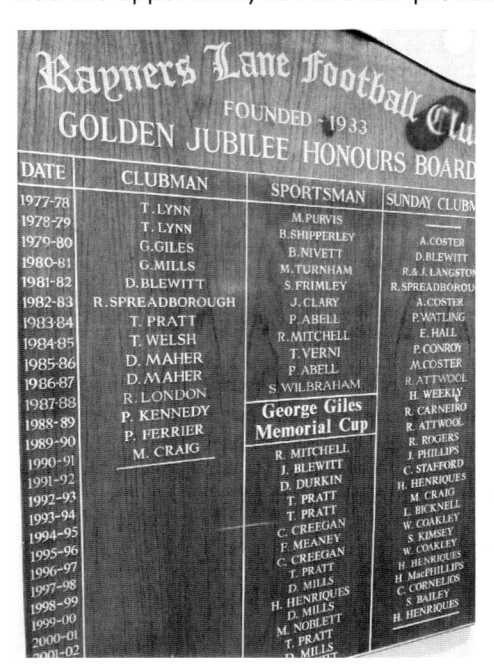

The Chairman - Pete Singh - now in his second season as Chairman, started up a company 'Football Future Stars' in 2021. It's a youth system which runs U13/14/15/16/18's all under the club umbrella. Within 3 years some of the players have gone onto Academy football, in fact his own son Reece is in his second year at Leyton Orient, Ciaran Martin is at Portsmouth, and Lasrat Ghulamnabi is in the Arsenal U16's. It appears that this youth set up is unearthing talent in a short space of time. Proof is that in their first year, the U15's became National JPL champions beating Stockport County in the final. No mean feat against a much larger club.

The crowds, although low, are increasing as success is coming on and most of their revenue comes at the gate

They have a board with 7 members who annually apply for re election and pay their stewards(all 2 of them).

The ground grading requirements, due to promotion, require the club to have an additional 48 seats(currently they have 102). The plan is to extend either side of their main stand, to raise their back seats, and erect terracing on the other side, all under cover of course. Not forgetting the obligatory extra turnstile and toilet. This will be completed by March 2025.

The atmosphere in the dressing room is now upbeat after they sacked their manager, after winning only one game from their first seven this season! They now have a football style where they play from the back, with no long balls and played on the ground.

The club have a mid budget for this division, which is good for a newly promoted side, and Josh Bostock is the man who pays the players wages.

Working with the community, I've been informed, is by word of mouth, as they receive regularly 10 phone calls per week from the local community and schools to talk to certain players to play for their club. They don't just teach football but life skills here as well.

If they do get promotion to step 3, then there is potential to buy land, as they wouldn't be able to expand further at the ground due to the local neighbours stopping any potential development behind one of the goals.

The future looks very bright for this club so go and check out what they are doing before they move when they get promoted again!.

ROMFORD V SPORTING BENGAL UNITED
ESSEX SENIOR LEAGUE PLAY OFF FINAL
06/05/24

Typical Bank Holiday Monday weather, chucking down with rain in time for the cup final. Yes, it's the Essex Senior League(step 5) play off final - Romford FC v Sporting Bengal United.

Is it going to be on or off? Half an hour before KO and it looks like a committee meeting is being held in the centre circle discussing the pitch condition! The goalmouth in the area nearest the turnstiles is full of mud & rain, but have seen worse this season at FC United of Manchester and the game still went ahead, albeit with tons of sand spread all around.

Romford's main aim this season is promotion to the Isthmian North Division - in speaking with Chairman Steve Gardener - however, unprecedented success is about to happen as they are in the League cup final in 2 days time, and 3 days after that the final of the FA Vase at Wembley! No mean feat for a team with a new manager and a new ground at the beginning of the season.

Romford in their home strip of all blue, plus yellow stripes on the top and shorts, and Bengal in green/red/green to kick off. Essex v East London. Incessant early Romford pressure put Bengal on the back foot, including goal line clearances. Until it settles down into a more even contest. On 34 mins it's Jay Knights glancing header which makes it 1-0 to Bengal. 42 mins a goal for Romford but ruled out for offside. 45 + 3 mins Romford hit the post, then a minute later they have a shot headed off the line. Bengal survive going 1-0 up. 10 mins into the second half and another glancing header makes it 0-2 against the run of play. 2 mins later, the Romford keeper comes out for a ball, misses it, and Bengals no.7 side foots into an empty net for 0-3. 5 mins later it's now 1-3 with Romford's no.11 getting one back. With 10 mins left a brilliant acrobatic save by the Bengal keeper tips over for another corner. An excellent defensive display from Bengal gets them over the line and promotion to the Isthmian North Division. At least it was a Bank Holiday bonanza with a crowd of over 1,000.

How many grounds have Romford played at of late? Well, they reformed in 1992, playing at Hornchurch. Since then they have had 6 'permanent' home and 15 more grounds since then! East Thurrock United folded at the beginning of season 2023/24. The owners of that now defunct club advertised their ground with a local estate agent which the club saw, took up, and are on a short to medium term lease, till they find another ground! This current ground is 17 miles from Romford, not ideal but feels like home now with their support. Crowds are on the increase now to 100-130(which was higher than before)due to the renewed interest and current success. Against Lincoln United, in the FA Vase semi final, the attendance was 600.

The community - its a real challenge to get youth teams in Romford here due to the distance. They have ladies/girls teams playing at all different places, and also have a cerebral palsy team - with a specialist coach on 3G - now that's a first in non league football. They play in tournaments with very relaxed rules. The end game is to get a team in a competitive manner.

The recent men's team success is due to the manager Dan Spinks, who has combined youth and experience together, but has a group of players who "will run through a brick wall" with their mentality, not literally of course! Dan was promoted from within previously being the assistant manager. Three to four of the current first team have come from the U18's so a steady progression of youth coming through.

Yes its nice to win the FA Vase but their main aim is promotion back to step 4 - The Isthmian North Division. It just goes to show the strength of this seasons Essex Senior with both finalists in the FA Vase coming from this Division.

As for the ground, the club rent from the owner and its on a rolling lease as he will eventually sell, more than likely to develop.

The club have improved the facilities within the bar and clubhouse with new flooring and have 2 bars. Update - the club are now based at Barking FC for this season.

RUSHALL OLYMPIC V BISHOPS STORTFORD
NATIONAL LEAGUE NORTH

09/04/24

A nice 3 hour, or so, journey along the usual motorways and into the West Midlands....and yet another gem of a club, this time in the National League North. It's a real family run club with fantastic hospitality - welcome to Rushall Olympic - a club that have won the Southern League Central play offs and two cups last season. Tonight hosting that other 'Northern' club, from just norf of London(!) namely Bishops Stortford. A must win game in the fight against relegation for Rushall, although not for Stortford as they are already confirmed as relegated.....and Rushall go 1-0 up in the 1st minute from no.17 Harry Palmer, sorry Owen Farmer(on loan from Wolves). Just getting used to the accents here from the announcer! Then 2-0 after 29 mins from Owen Oseni(on loan from Derby), which is how it stood at HT. Into the second half and you had no.3 for the away side Akolbire sent off with a second yellow. Life got easier thereafter with a third from Oseni, and his second, followed by a fourth from Joe Butlin. 4-0 to the Pics, as they're known, and they've now won 3 games on the trot to steer clear of relegation. They're using the on loan system wisely and have 2 more players in from Birmingham City and Walsall.

In speaking with Chairman John Allen, the club are very ambitious and have been expanding their building plans at the ground. Unfortunately the current ground lies on limestone mines. This has caused for two of the covered seating sections, opposite each other, to be moved further down towards both ends of the corner flags where they would be more stable. The far end goal is currently being developed to cover the length of that area, giving both covered seats and terracing. There is seating for 250 as required by the ground grading rules at this level. This will be completed by the end of April(extended deadline date). This new development can go ahead as it's at a low risk part of the ground. Updating the LED floodlights is also a basic requirement at this level.

However, the club is not standing still and it's ambitions will want to take them higher. Therefore they will eventually have to move as they couldn't build any further to accommodate their future plans. They are currently in "active discussion with the local authority and they (local authority) are responding".

They will look to move within Rushall, or slightly further afield, as they are looking at a minimum capacity of 4,000. They need to grow the club to afford to be in that division of capacity.

Behind the other goal is where the clubhouse/bar, and boardroom, are along with toilets, club shop and turnstiles. Along side both lengths of the pitch, you have to the left a long covered terraced area, as well as a disabled area. Opposite this side you have a long wooden and glass structure for the sponsors lounge. Named the Allen Suite, and dedicated to John's(Chairman)mother who died during covid. Next to that you have a tall gantry ready for the match of the day cameras, followed by the 'conservatory' control room - for directors and press. Outside here was where I had a chat with another Allen, son Nick, who is vice chairman. Nick informs me they have a great manager in Liam McDonald, who not only oversaw the winning of the league in the division below(the Southern Premier Central), but also won the treble winning 2 cups as well.

The 3G pitch is open 7 days a week, used by the local community and obviously generates great income for the club. The new stand being built, that I mentioned, is being funded by director Graham Jones to the tune of £250K, which I'm sure will look great when finished. The club President and Vice Presidents, Edwin Venables and Dave Greenwood(his brother Brian was a founder member)inform me, whilst speaking in the boardroom, that the club originated back in the 1890's(sometime prior to the 1893/94 season. However, even earlier records have indicated that football in the village of Rushall was already being played on a regular basis at least 20 years prior to that time, and in fact the opening game for the newly formed Walsall Town was against a Rushall side at the Chukery Ground, Walsall in October 1874. The team apparently changed in the local chip shop and walked to the park to play. The ground was originally a farmers field in an industrial area. Don't you just love these old stories!

Jumping ahead to the 1951, when they reformed after disbanding prior to WW2, and playing their first match v Walsall Swifts. They have been at their current ground since the 70's and the existing floodlights and cables were dismantled from the nearby Perry Barr speedway and taken to the new ground. The current clubhouse has been converted from what was a former bungalow. When they opened the ground at Dales Lane in 1977, a number of old Leeds players turned up for this including Jackie Charlton & John Charles…and they once had Allan Clarke play for them as a 'ringer' whilst playing at Leeds! You won't find these stories on Wikipedia!

The 1979/80 season saw the club win the 1st Division by a massive 16 points and promoted to the Premier Division of The Staffordshire County League. In 1994/95 the club were one of 20 founder members of the Midland Football Alliance. 2001/02 manager John Allen became Chairman but soon came back to manage in August 2003, which he's done a few times. 2004 saw major construction work and that season saw the club win the League and promoted to the Southern League Division 1 West. 2005/06 and a Staffordshire Senior cup win over Stoke City by a single goal at Stokes ground was the highlight.

2008/09 - restructuring of the Leagues saw the club moved to Northern Premier League 1st Division South. 2010/11 saw the club win promotion, via the play offs, to step 3 for the first time in their history beating Grantham Town in the final. Now we come to the present League of which they were promoted to last season in 2022/23, to the National League North from the Southern League Premier Division Centra,l after a 4-3 penalty shoot out in the play off final over Nuneaton Borough in front of a 3,500 crowd.

The average crowd here is around 450 which has increased massively with the recent success they've had, which includes 60 season ticket holders.

Former players the club have seen the likes of are - Stan Collymore, Lee Sinnott, Alec Reid, and have recently sold top scorer Danny Waldron to Southend. A club that has been careful in planning on moving up the leagues, which has undoubtedly come with getting the right managers in along the way, and not forgetting volunteers like Margaret Cartwright in hospitality. Along with vociferous supporters like Wayne who follow the team home and away, they have a great band of people at the club.

SAFFRON WALDEN TOWN V STANSTED
PETER BUTCHER CUP

24/09/24

A local Essex Senior League derby tonight - Saffron Walden v Stansted, but instead of a league game it's the Peter Butcher cup.

This is a proper old school ground - wooden benches in the main stand, painted in the team colours of red and black. Opposite is the Paul Daw stand(named after the former Chairman), and dug outs in front of the seats. Behind the far goal is covered seating, and the near goal you have a covered walkway,along with the turnstiles, and club museum in a long cabin - displaying old memorabilia of all sorts. Worthwhile going for the museum alone! If the club gain promotion, then all they would need to upgrade would be an extra turnstile and toilet as they are in effect all geared up for step 4 football.

Saffron Walden is a club that should be higher than their current step 5 status, playing at the Meadow, the same ground for the past 152 years and the best ground in this League! Chairman, Jamie Sharp, says the club need stability before promotion and getting crowds back to the 350 level. They have a great youth system in place from U7's to the A team reserves and 1st team, all having facilities including local and village space. There is a 3G pitch at the local school of which the FA have been great at providing help including 80% of the cost. There is also a 10 x 4m mini football pitch at the back of the ground, providing facilities for kids training. They're looking at bringing it back to the community, starting up the reserve team again and making a stance here by bringing in Dan Spinks from Romford, a top scorer last season.

Under the current chairman's stewardship, the floodlights are being replaced, which is ironic as Jamie's grandfathers first job at the club was to install the original floodlights! The club has raised £25K for the current lights, basically by Jamie's business contacts paying £5K x 5 companies. Plans are afoot to replace the East stand with £200K coming from the FA, the club have got £100K and just need to raise the same again to go ahead, probably in 2 years time. A new sprinkler system has also been installed.

The nickname of the club is the bloods, the same as Droysden. Both clubs have had joint pin badges sold with this on, which is unique, and quirky at the same time. One of their former famous players - Stewart Wardley - went to QPR for a fee of £15K, and then in his first season there scored 15 goals and was their player of the season.

Jamie describes the sponsors at the club as massive with their main sponsor being Saffron Walden Building Society. This along with 4 others that commit to annually sponsor the club - Garratts, Saffron Vantage,The Plough, Thaxted Stoves. They also have 35 banners around the ground at £350 per company.

Behind the scenes the club helps charities namely Chesterford Nursery, holding a charity match for them and raising £1,000. They cover a remembrance day for people locally, and help with mental health by bringing along celebrities like Jamie O'Hara to help bring in funds.

A money spinner for the club this summer was the Euro's. By having a big screen on the pitch they raised £15K at the tills, and on the day of the final it was sold out, a lock out, and you had people climbing over the walls to get in! Volunteers are not just a big part of the club, but the very foundation of the club.

As for the Game its Charlie Morris who draws first blood(excuse the pun!)on 18 minutes. Darren Phillips makes it 2 on 35 minutes, and then Roman Campbell gets the 3rd and 4th goals on 38 & 45 minutes to make it 4-0 at HT. There could have been a couple more in the second half but Saffron settled for a 4-0 home win and through to the next round of the cup with a mid week attendance of 181.

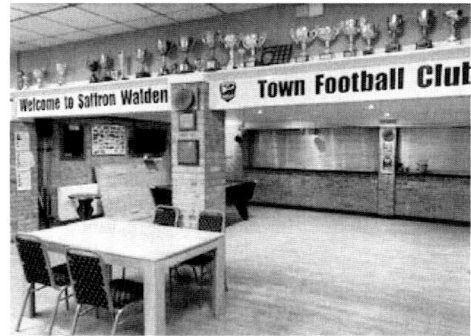

SCARBOROUGH ATHLETIC V ALFRETON TOWN
NATIONAL LEAGUE NORTH

20/04/24

A nice 9 hour return journey to the North Yorkshire coast to see Scarborough Athletic v Alfreton Town, in this end of season National League North encounter. A journey taking in the M11/A1/M18/M62/A614/B1249, as my game 82 of the season! Alfreton still in the play offs whilst Scarborough safe in mid table. Still, expecting a healthy crowd here today of 1,700.

In speaking with Chairman Trevor Bull, from this 100% fan owned club, "the club play at a level that they can afford to play at". Very wise words from a club that is well managed and run. HT and the away team are 1-0 after 28 mins as the goalkeeper misjudged the ball and went in over his head. Plenty of chances went begging from both sides but ultimately Alfreton just deserved their 1-0 win to send their party dressed up fans away singing. A decent crowd today of 1,835 with 164 away fans.

As for the ground - The main stand is all covered seating with great views of the countryside and hills around. At the top of the stand you have the sponsors lounge, boardroom and facilities. Opposite is the new seated covered stand, running the length of the pitch. The ground is all segregated with turnstiles at opposite ends of the ground. Behind the far goal is the home supporters covered terracing, and behind that is the fan zone in a white covered marquee. It houses the bar at one end and a stage at the other with today a female singer. To the side of the covered terracing is the well stocked club shop. All of these areas are operated by volunteers. The opposite goal end houses the away fans and to the right of them, and adjacent to the main stand, you have this 51 seater stand specifically for the away fans. Maybe its for 50 fans plus the coach driver?!

The original Scarborough club were formed in 1879. Today's current club is the Phoenix club reformed in 2007 and is a continuation of the old club. The old club didn't pay their tax bills and owed £2.3M before folding. They spent big when they got promotion, which was their ultimate downfall having no money to keep going. The new club had already formed a trust for the club and soon sprang into action, getting set up in the North West Counties League, within weeks of the old clubs demise. They had funding set up and were ready to go. Their first friendly game set up they had a crowd of 400 so the interest was most definitely there, despite playing away from home, and outside of town, at Bridlington. They targeted themselves to break even with crowds of 250.

When they first started training they couldn't go ahead as someone had forgot to go and buy some balls! At least the players were in place. This groundsharing with Bridlington lasted 10 years as an exiled club. Then in 2017 they moved into their present ground, which was built, and owned, by the local council. The council also owned the old ground and they made sure that the old ground was saved for no other purposes than football until a new facility was set up in place.

That same year the club were promoted to the Northern Premier League, and started off with a capacity of 2,000. They now have over a 3,000 capacity incorporating the new seated stand(opposite the main stand)and the 51 seater away stand. The ground, as mentioned, is segregated on police advice. The advice is basically you segregate, or we send in a load of police to the ground each game at a cost to the club. It's cheaper in the long run to segregate!

The club is 100% fan owned. Each member pays £15 per season on a one member, one vote basis. There are three different levels available at a bronze, silver, gold level of £15/20/30 but if you pay extra you don't get extra votes! The members currently total 1,645 and they hold AGM's & elections in November. Every 3 years board members have to stand for re election. The club are a non profit organisation. Their sponsors, of which they have 150, pay £300 per season. The club regularly communicate with them and also host an evening with sponsors, as a thank you, with an evening meal at a hotel. Chairman Trevor mentions that the club are fully self sustained. However, they can't generate income from the pitch as owned by the council. Their income is generated in match day through the turnstiles, sponsors, hospitality, bar, club merchandise. There is only one full time staff member - Rhiannon Hunt, who is doing a great job managing the club. Alongside volunteers like Bill I spoke to who watched his first game for the club v Northwich Victoria back in 1970 aged 3. He became a volunteer for the club in 1981. Stuart Bagnall, another volunteer, and a West Ham fan from Doncaster, who is one of the match day operators, informs me of their most famous managers namely - Colin Appleton who went to Leicester and then came back as a manager. Neil Warnock, who needs no introduction, but left the club having already lined up Notts County to go to in the background.

As for expansion plans, they will wait till they get promoted to step 1 before any further changes, if they were to get back into the football league. If they do, then it would be a 70% football foundation grant with the remainder coming from the club. As a Community Interest Trust, they have a strategy with 3/5/7 year plans for dealing with local schools, womens teams, and disabilities. The finance director of the club is Tim Rowe who runs the strategy of the club. A fascinating guy who has vast experience in dealing with football over seas in Finland, getting their main clubs in the Champions League,as well as in China, and Malaysia.

Their average crowds are 1500/1600. They rose from 1,000 back in 2017 and had 3,200 v Forest Green Rovers in the FA cup 1st round. They also have a 'sustainability fund' which has helped pay for the tarmac - to erect the white marquee tent with the bar, office, toilets, kitchen. In the main stand the club cannot use the well appointed kitchen. They have to use the now separate kitchen in the marquee. Prior to that they had to bring in food from outside! The funds raised to build the new stands came from the football foundation of £150K, and the club raised £50K. The council kept the naming rights to the stadium - Flamingo Land - but gave the money to the club as assets. The club officials are not allowed in during the week to the stadium as its run by the council. Therefore they operate the club from their own homes! Now that's a first I've never heard before. Any monies made goes to the the manager - Jonathan Greening - for his playing squad. Greening understands this, being a local lad, and formerly with WBA, Middlesbrough, Fulham, Man Utd. He also ran N. Forest U23's.

What does the future hold for Scarborough Athletic? Well, they are in a perfect position to stay where they are. If they were to reach the football league, they could build either side of the main stand to increase capacity. The council is now run by the North Yorkshire county council based in Northallerton.....and from next season they are going to re start the Anglo Scottish cup for fan owned clubs. They are called the Sea dogs, but no one from the officials or fans that I spoke to seem to know why! An old fisherman's tale? At least they're not called the seagulls.

SELSEY V ROFFEY
SOUTHERN COMBINATION LEAGUE DIVISION 1

28/10/23

Second game of the day down on the blustery Sussex coast and it's a proper ground - Selsey FC v Roffey. This time a Southern Combination League Division 1 fixture. A game that somehow survived the weather despite the torrential down pour throughout most of both halves.

Great meeting Chairman David Lee and all the officials of the Southern Combination League who took advantage of the groundhop weekend to give out free handbooks and badges.

I was enticed, prior to kick off, into the marquee tent, which was situated near the turnstile(singular), by the advert of veg curry with rice for a fiver. Absolute munch and just the job on a cold extremely wet, Saturday evening.

The first half shows a marked difference in the quality of football played in this division one game compared to the earlier game in division 2 watching Bosham FC. You can also see Roffey are a quality side and going forward they cruise into a 2 goal lead despite Selsey also looking good coming forward.

So, half time and back into the club house, to keep warm and dry, and have tea and cakes with the official's. It would be rude not to!

Second half and…..well a complete reversal of the first half. Once a Selsey player who had been knocked out and the offending Roffey no.9 sent off, the ref decided to send off no.8 as well. The away side 2-0 up but now down to 9 men. Then I was informed that the ref had operated the rarely used rule of sin binning the player for 10 mins.

Even so Selsey got a goal back straightaway. They pushed forward further to get an equaliser, but the rain didn't abait. The equaliser came and the game ended all square at 2-2, with thanks to the ref for keeping the game going when he could have taken the easier option and abandoned the game.

Selsey were actually formed in 1903, playing at various grounds until setting up in their High Street ground in the late 1940's, where the club remains to this present day, and which is now named the Seal Bay Resort Stadium after their sponsors. The ground was originally the gardens of a manor house which was left to the village of Selsey so that recreational sports could be played there. They were a formidable force in the West Sussex football league and dominated in the 1950's. Now to today playing a decent level of fluid attacking football.

They pulled out all the stops to have a record crowd of 327 attend with a great food choice, a good selection of club merchandise, programme, and a great clubhouse atmosphere.

They are a FA Chartered Standard Community club and is entirely run by a small number of volunteers from the local community and is a non profit making club.

The remit of Selsey FC is to develop young players, and alongside their U23 side, an U18 and U16 squad have been added to the ever increasing list of teams within the club, which includes a fully associated Selsey FC Women's team who play in the Women's National League Division 1 South West. There is also a successful reserves team made up of ex players and others affiliated to the West Sussex League. The Selsey Youth comprises at least 10 teams from ages 6 to U13.

Local well known ex professional player - Martin Hinshelwood - ex Crystal Palace player and Brighton manager, is also a 1st team coach there. The family have a strong professional footballing background and are a local Selsey family.

Check them out!

SHEFFIELD FC V NANTWICH TOWN
FA CUP EXTRA PRELIM ROUND
03/08/24

First competitive game of the season and it's the FA Cup extra prelim round. Home to the worlds first football club Sheffield FC, as recognised by FIFA, who today take on Nantwich Town.

The club were formed in 1857 as they were originally a cricket club, and as the first ever football club they played amongst themselves. They started out as a cricket and athletics club, and formed a football club to keep fit in the winter! Their first games were married men v unmarried men and they eventually persuaded another local cricket club - Hallam - to form a football club(which happened in 1860) so they would have another team to compete against! THE CLUB, as they are known, have a project called the Pioneers. This is designed to play, and have a link to, the oldest clubs in different counties round the world. This is giving the club worldwide reach and exposure.

They also have an aim and that is to educate. The club are well embedded in the local community with youth, girls, ladies, disability teams, and all inclusive, of which they have one of the biggest in the country. They were also the first team, (this club is indeed a succession of firsts!) to tour North America in 1904. This was titled the 'Pilgrims tour' and covered the East coast of both Canada & America.

Speaking with Chairman Richard Tims, who informs me that he took over back in 1998. At the time he was a disillusioned Sheffield Wednesday fan and took on the responsibility of taking the club from crowds of one man and his dog to an average now of appx 400. They previously played at Don Valley stadium but the club needed promoting and with Richard's background in marketing and print, helped steer them in the right direction and also move them to their present ground here in Dronfield, Derbyshire, just on the border with Sheffield and South Yorkshire. Moving to this ground named 'The home of football', was the clubs first permanent home in 140 plus years.

Their new ground, which will be in Sheffield, will be in appx 2 years time. It's only a mile up the road and they are just waiting upon a planning decision as plans have already been submitted. The capacity will be 5,000 and similar in design/scale to Boston United. To quote Pele, from 2007, "Without Sheffield FC there wouldn't be me!" The quote that's seen on the back of buses around Sheffield! The final score was 2-1 to the home side, after being 1-0 up at half time, and Sheffield now play away to Clitheroe in the next round - the Prelim round - of the FA cup. Attendance today is 318.

SOLIHULL MOORS V WEALDSTONE
NATIONAL LEAGUE

31/08/24

A 3 hour drive to just outside Birmingham for today's National League game between Solihull Moors and Wealdstone.

A club formed in recent years between a merger of 2 clubs in 2007, namely Moor Green & Solihull Borough. The club have been playing here since their merger which is about 8-9 miles away from the town centre and only 6 miles from Birmingham City's ground. Speaking with Director of football - Stephen Ward - an ex pro with the likes of Wolves, Burnley, Stoke, Ipswich, and an international with Ireland. The Ethos here is that its a real family club with a community feel to it. The club are in their infancy and still building. Of course their vision is to get into the football league, being sustainable at the same time. The past two seasons they haven't been far off with last season missing out in the play offs, and losing in the FA trophy final both at Wembley. 'Wardy', as he's affectionately known, has taken a different route from finishing playing at a high standard, to take a masters degree in sports directorship.

His remit is now overseeing transfer recruitment, coaching staff, and is a link between manager and chairman with the style of play. He is basically involved in every facet of the football club, which he loves coming to work every day. Trevor Steven's was the former President, going back to 2007, who was the main instigator with the merger of the clubs back then, and it wasn't until 2018 that current Chairman - Darryl Eales - came in. In 2015/16, the club got promotion to the National League. Unexpectedly, as the club were 12 points adrift at the bottom of the table by Christmas 2017/18, they turned things around and this amazing transformation led them to win the league with a game to spare.

Darryl mentioned that it is challenging here but made easier due to the high standards they set - positivity is just in built with the officials and players of the club. The key part of recruitment of players is that it's ingrained into the culture of the club. They are 'punching above their weight' compared to their rivals in this division due to not as much history, yet have a heart of gold with everyone I spoke to. To quote Darryl, "A club with purpose, heart and soul, more than just football".

The facilities are second to none at this level. The ground itself is looking very much like a football league ground, and their philosophy is 'bringing everyone together rather than an 'us and them attitude'. They have no boardroom as the facilities are used by everyone together - A refreshing attitude indeed. The crowds here, over the last 5 years, have quadrupled with an average of

1600/1700, and U12's coming in for free. They are slowly building their fan base with this infrastructure and their success on field. Most expansion plans have already been fulfilled, and they are surrounded here by Jaguar, Land Rover plants. The council have stated that land here is suitable for employment and potentially, in 3-5 years time, due to potential acquisition of the land, the club could relocate as they have looked at a number of sites near the M42/NEC areas. This will happen WHEN(not if)they get promoted. Any finance would come from the sale of the stadium plus from the likes of the council/Sport England. The area would be on a smaller scale with a shopping centre and hotel attached.

As for their youth, they have 60 teams via their foundation, along with an academy development(elite) - U16 to U18 with at least 3 players on the bench today to come through this route. So, a clear pathway from youth to the 1st team. Alongside these there are also 3 disability and 6 womens teams. The training ground facilities also houses their education for the academy - 2 grass pitches, a gym(as good as most league clubs), which is a great attraction to potential new players.

As for the game, the Moors had a few chances in the first half not put away, until they took control and finally in the 40th min. it was James Gale, a young striker, who rose high to head in from a corner. 1-0 at HT. However, early in the second half it was Wealdstone who equalised with a deflected shot. A game of two halves then and the points shared.

SOUTH SHIELDS V DARLINGTON
NATIONAL LEAGUE NORTH

17/02/24

Ha'way the Mariners it is as oop norf, here in South Shields, in this local derby v Darlington. South Tyneside v Co.Durham. An eagerly anticipated clash with the claret and blues, only 3 points from the play offs, facing the black and white Quakers who are sadly in the relegation zone at present. A club with a lorra fantastic canny people here, both staff(volunteers)and fans alike. The ground is looking great here at the I Cloud arena(formerly Filtrona Park) after gradually being built around since 2015 when current chairman - Geoff Thompson - bought the lease out and has built a fabulous 'Rocket stand' complete with bar, clubhouse, club shop, boardroom, all underneath this main stand. The players tunnel is opposite situated where the Durata covered stand is - standing & seats - alongside a new marquee accommodation with bar and at the other end, on the same side, is more covered terracing. Unusually there are covered terracing behind both goals for a non league team at this level. One of those areas houses the away fans, and is segregated but with the home fans adjacent to them! Darlington are expected to bring appx 300 fans today in a crowd of appx 2,800, which will be their biggest crowd of the season. The floodlights are unique in as much as reflect the club colours of claret and blue on both sides of the outer rims - West Ham take note! The facilities are second to none at this level - with hospitality at the Shipley's restaurant. Close by is the function room with another 2 bars. There is a fanzone towards the corner flag of one of the sides, and at the back of that away stand. The club also houses a 3G pitch which the juniors play on.

A fairly packed crowd today with both sets of fans noisily singing away throughout the game....Shields are first to put the ball in the net but ruled out for offside after 7 mins. Then in the 10th min no.8 Robert Briggs gets a red card for a deliberate foul on the last man on goal. 37 mins gone and play stops for the injured Darlo keeper whilst he receives treatment(magic sponge?!) Into the second half at 0-0, yet Darlo piling on the pressure with their extra man. It pays off in the 71st min as the away side go 0-1 up which rebounds out for a simple header in. 4 mins later and it's 0-2. Then 85 mins and a 2nd sending off for the home side who are now obviously down to 9! Right at the end of normal time, the away fans are treated to a third, and right on 94 mins it's 0-4 from no.20 Curry.

Back to a packed clubhouse for a live band - the Monday Club - serving up known favourites from Joy Division, Clash, Blur, before the long journey back down to SE London.

The history of a proud club formed in 1888 and re founded in 1974. Originally starting out as South Shields Athletic AFC playing in Mowbray Road. The first 'real' football club to bare its home town name. Another club existed without the AFC tag, alongside South Shields Adelphia Argyle and South Shields Albion, then in 1895 South Shields AFC(late congregational). The club was a member of the Northern Alliance League for 5 years, before being disbanded due to finance problems. Other clubs that were around at the time - South Shields United, South Shields YMCA, South Shields Argyle, South Shields Borough United, South Shields Villa, South Shields Celtic, South Shields Albion Star!! They first went into the football league in 1919 as South Shields Adelaide Athletic - I'm sure they made these names up as they went along! 1908/09 - they operated at the Horsley Hill ground, with their home colours of red and green. The maritime connotations being the colours of port and starboard. 2 years later they changed to South Shields FC. The few years prior to WW1 were the most successful in the clubs history, winning the championship 2 years running, admitted to full membership of the FA, and runners up to Darlington in 1912. The following season they scored 160 goals with centre forward Irvine Thornley scoring 70 goals(eat your heart out Alan Shearer!). 1922 - they sold Warney Cresswell to Sunderland for the then league transfer fee record of £5,500 - the only international to ever play for the club.

24,348 - is the ground record attendance achieved in 1926/7 when they played Swansea in the cup. 1930 - they moved to Gateshead to save themselves from bankruptcy. However, in 1936, a new club emerged in the town and joined the North Eastern League, based at the old ground in Horsley Hill. They played in red and green squares(the design of their kit that is!)and won the league in 1938/39. 1947 - In an FA cup game they beat Radcliffe Colliery Welfare 13-0 with Chris Marron scoring 10. 1950 - they moved to Simonside and produced a record attendance there of 30,500 and adopted the nickname of the Mariners. Between 1958 & 1968, they were in 4 different leagues, culminating in joining the Northern Premier League as a founder member. 1970 - they reached the 3rd round of the FA cup losing to QPR. 1974 - was a year of turmoil moving away from the town and re emerged as Gateshead United. What emerged locally was South Shields Mariner's FC(hence the reformation of a complicated history of the club).

1992 - the ground of Filtrona FC became available and was bought by the club chairman. Upgrading and promotion in the leagues followed. 2013 - the clubs lease on the ground expired and the club were forced to move out and go 20 miles down the road to Peterlee for 2 years. 2015 - New chairman Geoff Thompson stepped in and bought Filtrona Park renaming it Mariners Park(now 1st cloud arena). In the first season they won the Northern League Division 2 with 107 points, also along the way winning the FA vase, and a 3rd consecutive league title, narrowly missing out on a 4th losing in a play off final. Covid denied them promotion in those two intervening years.

The rest is history now in this 9 year period with massive ground improvements, alongside the share scheme which went on to raise £380,000 as 1,000 people became shareholders. Current Operations director - Carl Mowatt - is also a fantastic ambassador for the club introducing myself to the unique international academy the club run. This is for mostly overseas American and Mexican students studying for Masters degrees and being trained and looked after here by the club. Playing in the academy league against the likes of Man City U23's. All coaches are UEFA licenced and players train 2/3 times a week. This ultimately, is building up a reputation for the club raising awareness globally. One of their own up and coming stars - Joao Gomes - a Portuguese player, is one from their graduate academy. The club are also willing to take on board Uni students to become volunteers, yet get valuable training regards the media side of the club, such as Ben Marston and Dom Aberdeen. Not forgetting other volunteers such as Sue in hospitality and Jackie in the club shop. The chairman Geoff, is currently looking to sell the club due to health and family reasons. This will look to take the club onto the next level.

SOUTHEND UNITED V MAIDENHEAD UNITED
NATIONAL LEAGUE

19/09/23

Over to the Essex coast tonight for a National League game - Southend United v Maidenhead United.

One team battling for survival and I'm not talking relegation here. Dire times for Southend and unless they can come up with a buyer for the club, before the 4th October(their last court case) then they no longer exist! Let's hope for the club, and especially their loyal supporters that this can happen and they do indeed get a buyer.

Anyway, the ground itself is looking a tad run down to say the least - barrel vaulted roofs on one side of the ground and also behind the goal. An all seater stadium it is, so apart from the aged look, a proper league ground. Sitting along the half way line so a good view to be had from the directors seats - although they look like the original seats, solid wood and metal. No non environmentally friendly plastic rubbish in this part!

Straight from the KO the chants go up 'We want Martin out'(the much loved chairman Ron Martin!)

Crowd here of 4,748 with 43 away fans....and on 26 mins the crowd throw on a mixture of toy rats & tennis balls. The rats are a new one to me - perhaps symbolising the chairman!

The ref calls the players off a couple of times then after that short delay, more chants go up of 'Martin's a w***** everywhere he goes'!

Southend only have 2 subs left from their 16 man squad, so hopefully no more injuries over the next few games otherwise they'll be the first professional club playing with less than 10 men!

So to the crowd who are getting rowdier and security dragging a few out. To HT and no score with more excitement coming from the crowd.

Second half and it'sin the 73rd min with a penalty to Southend. Jack Bridge blasts it into the top middle emphatically. 1-0 to the Shrimpers and there is still life in this 118 year old club!

Then in the 91st minute, a superbly taken goal from Wesley Fonguck. He took on two players then swerved it into the far corner to make the final score 2-0. The players did a 'lap of honour' at the end and you'd thought the team had just won the league with the reaction of the fans!

The club were originally formed in May 1906 at the Blue Boar Hotel after the landlord invited a group of businessman and footballers to discuss setting up a new professional club. This new club would displace Southend Athletic who later disbanded. The club won the Southern League 2nd Division in its first two seasons, then being admitted to the Football League in 1920. They spent the next 44 years in the third tier of the League before dropping into the 4th Division in 1966. Jumping ahead to 1991 they were finally promoted to the 2nd Division(now the Championship)where they stayed for 6 seasons. Then they had a double relegation in 1997 & 1998......then won a double promotion back again in 2005 & 2006. The club don't do things by half! Then another double relegation in 2020 & 2021 and ultimately dropping out of the Football League.

As we type the club is still in the balance and we don't know yet whether the club will survive or start afresh as a phoenix club.

ST IVES TOWN V KETTERING TOWN
SOUTHERN LEAGUE PREMIER CENTRAL
09/09/24

A Monday night game in Cambridgeshire and it's St Ives Town v Kettering Town from Northamptonshire. A Southern League Premier Central clash, two days after seeing Royston over come Kettering in this division.

St Ives stride out in their black and white shirts and black shorts, to a decent mid week crowd with plenty of away support from Kettering. The club were originally founded in 1887, have been at this ground since the 1960's - prior to that it was the Meadow Lane ground which was gravel. The current ground was formerly a farmers field and orchard prior to the conversion to a football pitch. However, it's been renowned for previously being the worst pitch in the league with 4-6 inches of top soil on top of 1 metre of clay. In wet weather, at least 4 games a season were called off and in the dry summer weather the pitch cracked up (quote) "like a jigsaw puzzle!"......until the recent installation of their 3G pitch.

This has been their key to financial sustainability, allied with the generous annual continuous support of their sponsors who support the club. The club has been transformed from 1 team to now 21 teams overall due to this new pitch. At least the club own their ground and stadium outright. The 3G pitch has been financed by both Paul Reason(chairman)and Gary Clarke(director)to the tune of over £500K which incidentally was far less than the £800K quoted by the FA. The greed at the FA get there quotes farmed out by 'consultants', who make £thousands from the club and then want to have control over the income that comes in. As well as wanting a seat on the board of directors of each club. Unbelievable - helping out small non league clubs? I don't think so! With this pitch they also have a far better quality one than that quoted by the FA, which includes shock absorbers underneath the pitch.

The main clubhouse, with covered standing outside, also backs onto the hospitality area for away directors, the players tunnel, and turnstiles. Opposite is the main covered seated stand and either side you have two Mick George stands - one seated and the other standing, but both covered. Behind both goals are open walkways. They are probably at the level which is now sustainable for them, before embarking onto promotion to the next step up to the National League North.

Game on in the first half with a cracking well taken goal by St Ives put the home team 1-0 up, 6 mins before the end of the first half. Into the second half and eventually Kettering get an equaliser via a penalty…..and near the end what looks like the winner as it's now 1-2. Attendance of 471, and their average crowds have been 350(increased from 280 the previous season).

This has been a rapid progression for the club from step 5 to step 3 of which this is now their 3rd season in this division. The club organize collections for charities including fireman's, local cancer, and organize a football boot exchange for youngsters who can't afford a new pair of boots. Maureen Clarke, wife of Gary, is now finance director, as well as running the academy division of boys teams. She only came along with her husband 20 years ago and got roped in to volunteer due to her finance experience! Along with Mark, the chef, they also ensure the lads in the academy are well fed with mid day meals.

TADLEY CALLEVA V WOODLEY UNITED
COMBINED COUNTIES PREMIER DIVISION CUP

09/05/24

Tonight's League cup game throws up a Step 5 v step 6 in the non league pyramid with a Hampshire v Berkshire feel to it.

Tadley have been going since the early 1900's, originally on a park pitch. They used to be Tadley FC and reformed in 1989 as Tadley Town, with the help of Murray Knox(who now runs the bar). Then in 2005, Tadley Town amalgamated with Calleva boys club to secure a proper ground for adult football. In 2007 they secured their current ground and subsequently built it up to the current position in step 5, which incidentally is the highest position they've been in, finishing 4th this season and just losing out in the play offs. They were promoted from step 7 in the Hants league to step 6, then in 2017/18 promoted to step 5 in the Wessex Premier League. The Hants League amalgamated with the Wessex League Division 1 where they were for 17 years. The Wessex League is now the Combined Counties North with the FA restructuring of the Leagues. Subsequently the club 'moved' to the Combined Counties South and will be coming into their third season now(highest position).

They did win the Wessex League in 2007/08 but weren't promoted due to ground grading being not sufficient at the time.

The ground capacity is 1500 and their biggest attendance was against AFC Bournemouth in an FA cup game with a crowd of 700.

Plans are afoot to add an additional seated stand, another turnstile, and the kitchen is under redevelopment next to the bar. Further building will be for 6 changing rooms and toilets.

As for the ground itself, the club do not own it but sub lease it. They do own the facilities though.

Sandy(Alexander)Russell - chairman - started with the club in 1994 as assistant reserve manager. He ran the 1st team in 2000-2003 before becoming chairman in 2010.

The name Calleva is an old Roman name, taken from the nearby Roman town of Calleva Atrebatum, and their nickname funnily enough is the Romans being not too far from Silchester an old Roman camp.

Tadley Calleva adopted the name as a nod to the heritage and roots of the town and surrounding areas. This can be visibly seen on their badge with the Roman gladiator between two besom brooms, which are famous to the town of Tadley. So now you know!

The success of this club is down to the people behind the scene who have built the club up to where it is now, both sustainable and self sufficient. They have their own facilities successfully running the clubhouse, bar, and new kitchen about to be built as mentioned.

The current ground was donated to the club by John Stacey & Sons co.(George Stacey the MD), but owned by Basingstoke council on a 100 year lease. Its leased to Barlows Park(sublet). This is the best position the club has ever been in both with the football side and in running the club. Prior to this in 1992/93, Geoff White and Ray Dobson managed to get a lot of the funding - £1.6m - to fund the ground.

2014 - One of their most renowned games. Just mention Basingstoke, their near noisy neighbours (of step 3) whom they beat in a cup game when they were at step 6. Basingstoke were the holders, at that time, of the Hampshire Senior cup. The club managed by Jason Bristow (now gone on to Eastleigh) took 200 fans to the ground as is forever remembered.

In 2015/16 they beat Chertsey, Littlehampton, and Newport(IOW), in the FA Vase and in 2018/19 lost out to eventual winners Chertsey.

The youth teams are separate to the club and they also have U18, U23 and vets sides affiliated.

The financial backing of local businesses and individuals has been, and will continue to be, vital to our on and off field successes. We would like to put on record our sincere gratitude to A4 Metal Recycling Ltd for their long term and continued support of the club, as well as a number of other local businesses.

The game itself - 5 mins gone and the away side go 1-0 up. A lot of Tadley pressure but no home goals as yet. Then on the stroke of HT it's 1-1. 14 mins into the 2nd half, and it's time for Tadley to take the lead this time. The floodlights, on one side of the pitch, go out in the second half, and the ref stops the game. One by one the light bulbs eventually come to life. Tadley are 2-1 up by now and likely to reach the next round, of which the winners play Langley, in the quarter finals at Uxbridge's ground. Near the end though more drama ensues as the game is stopped again this time due to some 'arguments' on the touchline. An away fan is asked to leave as he had punched a home player on the touchline! Unbelievable. After it all calms down a game of football breaks out! 2-1 at the final whistle it is then.

TRING ATHLETIC V AYLESBURY VALE DYNAMOS
SPARTANS SOUTH MIDLAND PREMIER LEAGUE

20/08/24

Over to Tring Athletic, at the Michael Anthony Stadium in Hertfordshire, for their home league local derby game v Aylesbury Vale Dynamos. This is step 5 in the Spartans South Midlands Premier League.

A ground set in countryside and alongside the rugby & squash clubs, with a 20 minute walk away from town. A really picturesque ground with an old fashioned main wooden seated stand similar to Spalding. Adjacent to this is the clubhouse, bar, players dressing rooms. On the opposite side you have a small covered wooden seated stand with chequered red & black flags resplendent at each end. Behind one goal is a long covered terraced and seated area. Well the seats are all in a single line, screwed to a plank of wood and resting on top of columns four deep of breeze blocks. Unique non league architecture! At the other end it's an open walkway with a walk around a preserved tall tree practically behind the goal.

So far it's goalless, in this first half, due to a couple of great saves from both keepers. Tring are in red shirts and black shorts(hence the two coloured chequered flags around the ground), whilst Aylesbury are in blue/yellow shirts and blue shorts….Then Tring go 1-0 up early in the second half. A looping header makes it 2-0…..near the end, Aylesbury come back with 2 goals in 4 minutes to draw level at 2-2 with the points shared tonight.

Speaking with new Chairman Darrell Osborne, who has been in the hot seat now for two months, having only joined the committee 1 1/2 years ago. This is a man passionate about the club, having lived locally for the past 30 years and seeing his two children through from coaching up to U16, then coaching back youngsters from U6's once again!

The club were founded in 1958, and were originally just an U21 side. They moved to their present scenic setting in 2003(originally a greenfield site). They currently have plans submitted for a 3G pitch which, once laid, will be transformative to a club like this. The drainage here, like a lot of clubs, is bad to say the least and this in effect will cure the problem and bring welcome finance in as well. The clubhouse is used a lot for functions including the local nursery in the community. Their sponsors seem well looked after given a free gold card membership of the club. This also gives a lot of benefits for supporters with various discounts at the club. The club are focussing more on the local community now as well as getting an in road into the local schools to attract crowds as well.

Their current average crowd is around 150, and still increasing, with a capacity of appx 1,000. They recently played Bury FC in the FA Vase which attracted over 800. The club have the affiliation of Tring Tornadoes who have youth teams ranging from U6 to U16. Tring Athletic have an U18, U23, an A team(which is local lads ambitious for the U23's), a development team currently playing Sunday League and a mixture between U18 & U23's. Their youth section - they have a great affiliation with Tring Tornadoes, who are run as a separate club and a big club in their own right. They are currently creating more collaboration with this club and also give the opportunity for youth players to become mascots on match days.

Most famous player appears to have been Peter Gibbs, a goalie who went on to play for Watford in the 70/80's. From their batch of current players they have brothers Max & Frankie Hercules - their Dad played for local rivals Aylesbury who incidentally played England in a friendly in 1988!

Plans are afoot to enhance their boardroom, and create a club shop with a range of merchandise. With the enthusiasm of the new chairman, Tring will see exciting times ahead.

WARRINGTON RYLANDS V CHEADLE
PRE SEASON FRIENDLY

06/07/24

Todays friendly fixture is a 4 hour drive away and a 2pm KO(due to the England v Switzerland game later).

Welcome to the Hive Arena, home to Warrington Rylands who entertain Cheadle Town. Rylands are a club who've had a meteoric rise over the past 6 years. One of the directors I spoke to, Tony, informs me that the club, although originally formed in 1906 as Rylands Whitecross, and were a works team producing wire works and nails, had the junior club section set up in 2016 with 15 teams. In 2018 the club entered the North West Counties league Division 1 South, prior to playing in the Cheshire League at step 7. This was due to the restructuring of the Leagues at the time. They won this division at the first attempt and were promoted to the North West Counties Premier, at step 5, which they won again at the first attempt. The club were promoted on the PPG(Points per game system) during covid and effectively completed a 'double' by winning the FA Vase at Wembley. Then the 2021/22 season, at step 4 in the Northern Premier League Division 1 West, they won their division remarkably again in their first season. They consolidated their first season in the NPL Premier finishing 10th and last season lost out in the play off semis to Marine.

They have 4 directors - Tony Bennett, Mark Pye, Andy Martin, and Andy Hibbert. A well run club with a number of local sponsors who fund the club. Rylands currently have 32 teams, including ladies, and they create a pathway for the youth, from U7's, to the 1st team. Their first player(homegrown) to achieve this is Ben Taylor who now has a contract at the club. They have sold off a few players of late to football league clubs with the likes of - Elliott Nevett to Tranmere, then onto Crewe and now Gillingham. Kane Drummond to Chesterfield, and a real gem in Adama Sidibeh who has gone onto St Johnstone and now an international with The Gambia. Elliott Nevitt was their player who scored a hat trick at Wembley in their FA Vase win over Binfield in 2021.

Importantly the club also raises money for a local hospice and recently raised £2,500 for the local hospital. It's 'doing the right thing for the local community'. Admission fees currently are adults £10, concessions £7, children U16 £2. However, the youth team players get a free season ticket when they sign on, and free for 1 adult as well. A great way of introducing families into the club for the long term future. The crowds are now at an average of 520, whereas 6 years ago it was around 60!

Their meteoric rise is due to their Junior/pathway system and their work within the local community. The centre of excellence they have is run by Nicky Hunt(ex Bolton), and the next step is the education style of B Techs being offered through their links with local colleges. Interestingly, one of their main sponsors over these success years was Paul Stretford who is the football agent for Wayne Rooney &

Harry Maguire. Paul's father also has a seated stand at the ground named after him. Just so you know! They are now planning on moving within the next 2 years to bigger facilities and buying, then developing. I can't tell you where yet as not common knowledge! Ultimately they aim to get into the football league. Ambitious and proud of it!

Onto the game and it's 1-0 after 6 mins...in 39 mins a shot hits the bar then another shot is saved acrobatically by the Cheadle keeper. Within 2 mins of that it's 2-0. On 43 mins the No.11 is one on one with the keeper and proceeds to nutmeg him for the 3rd goal. Cheadle tightened up in the second half, scored a goal from their No.9, and Warrington kept the score to a 3-1 win.

As mentioned their history goes back to 1906 - and it took them 112 years as an amateur club before turning semi-pro in 2018. Back in 2008, Rylands FC merged with local rivals Crosfields FC playing under a joint name, until the two clubs split in 2012, and the name Rylands FC resumed. Prior to the 2020/21 season the club changed its name to Warrington Rylands FC. The name change was designed to help spread awareness of the club outside its local environs while ensuring the Rylands name would remain synonymous with the club, whilst also recognising the club had played and been a part of Warrington since 1906 and still playing on the original ground.

WARRINGTON TOWN V SOUTHPORT
NATIONAL LEAGUE NORTH

05/03/24

National League North midweek game tonight and over to the Cantilever Park, home to Warrington Town FC.

The club are newly promoted from last season and taking on the seaside town, and former league club, of Southport. A rearranged game as previously postponed due to the weather. Warrington are currently in a race against time to get their ground up to scratch for ground grading requirements, with the ominous threat of relegation if they don't!...don't worry, they will, get it completed that is! They have nearly completed a new seated area behind one goal, and this I've been informed, by long standing steward Andy, will be for the away fans. Purchased from Lincoln City and just the roof to go on then. The opposite end is where the home fans congregate under the covered terrace. The main stand, seated, (blue seats in this stand have come from Man City's old ground at Maine road) is on the opposite side to where the players come out - their changing rooms pitch side, and the referees area sandwiched in between. Above these rooms are the media announcer, the boardroom and the more modern hospitality/sponsors lounge. Alongside you have another pitchside lounge bar, 'Jackie's Baps' hot food van, and another small covered terrace.

Lots of yellow and blue around the ground - the home colours. Chairman, Toby Macormac, is busily sorting out the ground grading prior to organising tonight's game, so extremely busy more so. The stewards on the gate seem to love their job, all volunteers of course, and a healthy sign of a good club going forward. In the hospitality area, the food here is second to none with Quorn curry and at half time lemon meringue tart with cream. Sponsors get your bookings in now! Served up by Lisa Macormac and ably assisted by daughter Freya.

The fan base here are really noisy and vocal, mostly down to the youngsters behind the goal who are the 'under 5's(a West Ham connection then?!) A neatly packed out ground with attendance of 1,421, which is great for a re arranged game on a Tuesday. A few supporters from Southport tonight make the short trip from Merseyside to North Cheshire....and the away side go 1-0 up after 12 mins, then 2-0 after 38 mins. You wouldn't think you were watching 9th v 19th in the table as Marcus Carver scores with a sublime chip over the keeper. The latter part of the game Southport tie up with a 3-0 scoreline not before play was stopped near the end so the away keeper could get his head bandaged up after colliding with the post! All in all a fabulous club with a real community feel to it. When the turnstile operators - Amanda & Marie - unpaid volunteers tell you 'they love the club', then you know there's something special about the club.

The population of the town is 230,000 which incidentally is the 3rd highest population for a town, in the whole of the country that doesn't have a professional football team. I can see more and more fans coming along especially if they get success on the pitch. They'll soon need more terracing and seating to cope with the numbers!

The ground grading currently in place is the new stand, as mentioned, plus all the walkways around the ground to be concreted. The new stand has been a project since August 2023 to achieve grading 2(currently 3 at the moment). They now currently have 434 seats and looking to get 500 within 3 years of National League membership to meet the regulations. They will build another 100 seater stand in that time, which will be next to the main stand but haven't allocated a space yet. There are no plans afoot to change their grass pitch as the cost will be too prohibitive at appx £700K to a FIFA step 2 quality. Although Warrington is a rugby town with their ground holding 15,000, the football club are not competing against them as they're increasing their crowds within their own right. In fact appx 11 years ago the club had crowds of around 200. Now they regularly attract 1,100.

Most of the development work has been paid for from 3 main sources - fundraising from fans, the football foundation (68%), and the chairman himself. The junior teams have dropped off down from 28 to 17, but they now have an U18, U21, & ladies team in place. The chairman took over in 2009, got rid of the debt and changed to a limited company that year. It was previously run by a committee. You get the feel of a real family run club here, as well as the wider 'family' of dedicated volunteers that bring the club together.

The dedicated fans have recently completed a sponsored 40 mile walk to Altrincham and back, raising £9,000. This has been raised for the ground fund for upgrading. The stewards on the night have been fantastic with Phil, Andy, and Dave, keeping everything in check. Then you have the Warrington 'Loyal'. The fans who are there home and away - Keith Vernon, Adam Hesos, Mark Farnworth, Daz Kehoe, Mark Harper. Current players to look out for, and hopefully take them onto another level, are the likes of Sean Williams, Connor Woods who is an ex Southport player, Isaac Buckley-Ricketts, a striker, and Dan Atherton, a goalkeeper who has scored 2 goals this season and played in the champions league. What more could you ask for! Oh, and tonight's attendance was a mighty 1,421 on a cold midweek night.

WELWYN GARDEN CITY V BIGGLESWADE TOWN
SOUTHERN LEAGUE DIVISION 1 CENTRAL

11/04/24

Let's make a change tonight and go deep into Hertfordshire. Welwyn Garden City take on Biggleswade Town in a 6th v 1st encounter that has been rearranged after previous postponements. Welwyn are only 2 points away from a play off position with 3 games in hand. Biggleswade are on a roll at the moment flying at the top. Sounds like a cracking game on paper but Welwyn are being forced to play 4 games in 8 days over the next 2 weeks, to get the season completed. So, a tough ask here playing the top team. Promotion beckons for both sides to either the Southern Premier Central or the Isthmian League. Knowing the FA they'll probably get put in the National League North!

The Citizens, as they're known, play in all claret, with a smattering of sky blue, and were formed in 1921, the same time as the town was built. Biggleswade are in a fetching bright illuminous orange & black, so no need to turn the floodlights on tonight! Speaking with secretary Gavin Meaden, if they get promoted then they have to deal with the usual ground grading - extra turnstile and supply access, 150 more seats, and covered area for another 150 standing.....6 mins gone and it's the away team who are 1-0 up. 37 mins and it's 0-2. 56 mins and it's 0-3. A lot of play acting tonight and constant moaning from the away team which kinda spoils the game. Right near the end, a cracking shot smashes off the crossbar but still no goals for Welwyn. Tonights attendance was 165.

Back in 2017, Ozzie Ardiles came to the club to open the White Hart turnstile given to the club from Spurs, and other upgrades that happened at the time, including the opening of the two new stands and an improved clubhouse. This came about from a grant of £100K awarded from the Premier League, via the Football Stadia Improvement Fund.

The club own their own ground, and facilities which includes the 3G pitch and the clubhouse.

Former player of note is ex Spurs player Paul Price. Paul left Welwyn to join Luton initially in 1971. Another famous 'player'(if you call him that)is ex ref

Mark Halsey who was their goalkeeper for a time in the 1980's! Their current manager is Mark Weatherstone who is ex Wingate & Finchley, Dulwich Hamlet, and Enfield. Players to look out for are - striker Lynton Goss(ex Bedford), Dernell Wynter, Cyrus Babaio, and Brad Watkins the Captain. As always its the volunteers that keep the club going from the Chairman David Coates, to the bar staff and hospitality.

The club also run U15 youth and U18 Academy sides utilising the 3G training pitch for practice.

The club was originally formed in 1921 and the kit was red and white quarters. So, over a hundred years of football here and the same with this new grid designed 'Garden City'.

They were wound up in the 1935/36 season with debts of over £20!! In 1937, local rivals Shredded Wheat FC(seriously!) were wound up which allowed Welwyn, with a grant of £50 from the Shredded Wheat company, to be re-established. Finally moving into County football joining the Herts County League in 1959. The move to their present ground in Herns Way came about in 1968 and in 1970 they joined the Greater London League. The following season they became a founder member of the Metropolitan London League, then changed its mind after two seasons and joined the South Midlands League. 1972/73 - they merged with Welwyn Garden United to form Welwyn Garden FC. So to the mid 80's which saw them install floodlights at the ground. It wasn't until 2016/17 that extensive ground improvements were completed. The following season a club record 25 consecutive games unbeaten was set.

WHITBY TOWN V BASFORD UNITED
NORTHERN PREMIER LEAGUE PREMIER DIVISION
03/02/24

Over to the North Yorkshire coast today for another, soon to be, classic Northern Premier League Premier Division match between Whitby Town and Basford United(pronounced Baseford)from Nottinghamshire.

In a great interview with media man at the club, Paul Connolly, I get to find out about the club more in depth. Paul is now in his 10th season at the Town starting off as the programme editor.The club have a grass pitch which is holding up today after all the recent postponements due to the weather. This, like a lot of clubs, has proved detrimental financially and has cost the club in the region of £12/15,000 in lost revenue, which they can ill afford to lose.

Whitby, a proud club, can boast to have never been relegated...ever! The present club was a merger in 1926 between the two clubs Whitby Town and Whitby Whitehall Swifts, to become Whitby United. They then changed their name to Whitby Town in 1949, as well as changing their colours to red. They changed again in the mid 50's to an all blue top.

They have got through to a final at Wembley before, back in 1965, being beaten finalists to Hendon in the FA Amateur cup final. The majority of time has been spent in the Northern League. In 1993 the club applied to join the Northern Premier Division as a formality in winning the Northern League. However, the Northern League, and the FA, were complicit in not allowing Whitby to get promotion, as the Northern League wanted Whitby to stay in their League, as it was 'their day out when they went to their home games'. Unbelievable Jeff! The following season, I've been informed by a fan, the home programme had the Northern League on the front cover crossed out and replaced with the Northern Premier League, even though they were officially playing in the Northern League!

The unique point to their kit is that it is very similar to Sampdoria in Italy. Reason is their manager, at the time, was very much into 'Football Italia' during the 90's and liked Sampdoria! They copied the Sampdoria kit but Paul designed it so the the top, with the four colour stripes across it, had the black on top of the red rather than the other way round as at Sampdoria. So now you know!...so, to the game, and at precisely 2:39 the tannoy blasts out the Jam's 'Going underground'. Nice....great meeting up with Darlington season ticket holder Col Robson....

Players to look out for are - Junior Mondal, Dan Rowe (captain), Shane Bland who is renowned as the best goalkeeper in this division.

On 21 minutes, the sun shines even brighter here as the Town go 1-0 up via Junior Mondal who is back after suspension. Then a minute later, the Town keeper, Shane Bland, makes a spectacular save to stop Basford equalising, and turns it away for a corner. Chants of "Sea, sea, Seasiders" go up in the main stand. To the HT hospitality in the boardroom - well cooked Vegetable cottage pie presented by Mel Readman (a real diamond geezer), and a pint of John Smiths poured by smoove barman Mark!

Second half and yes a red for no.6 of Basford. Then we wait till the 81st minute for the goal of the season. Coleby Shephard, Whitby's left back receives a pass across midfield, turns 5 players inside out and calmly slots past the keeper for 2-0! Just into 5 mins added time and we have a penalty..calmly slotted in by Jacob Gratton to make it 3-0. Then we have another red card(2nd yellow)for Basford! A well deserved win for Whitby and not far off the play offs now. Three points in the bag and a crowd of 527.

Going back to 1995 - one of the floodlight pylons came down, and the club had to remove the rest as they were condemned. In 1996/97, this was the season they got promoted to their current division, and making it even healthier, they made a Wembley appearance storming through as 3-0 winners to defeat North Ferriby United and win the FA Vase.

Previous players of renown have been Eddie Gray, a former player and manager, as well as Peter Lorimer. Both former Leeds star players under Don Revie. Also Malcolm Poskett a goal scorer who went on to both Watford and Brighton, and not forgetting David Logan who went to Mansfield but came back in the mid 90's to become Whitby's manager.

The ground has a current capacity of 2,800 but is currently restricted to 1,200 by the local council. This was reduced after the crush barriers were removed on council advice. No money to replace, so it stays at that figure. Although their average crowd is around 500/600, this has increased substantially from the 250 they used to get 6/7 years ago. The increase is due to the club going into the community and schools, handing out free season tickets to schoolchildren.

Under 16's are always free with a paying adult. Adding to that a family section is designated in the main stand.

The impressive main stand was built, and ready for the 2005/06 season, with 500 seats. There are 4 floodlight pylons opposite the main stand and 2 others opposite that, with 2 smaller lights attached to the top of the main stand. The facilities encompass a large bar/clubhouse at the back of the main stand, with the boardroom and officials hospitality underneath that stand. The club shop is just to the side of it. They have a sponsors lounge further along, built from a reclaimed container - looks great inside - and run by sponsors director Scott Booth. Also provided are two canteens, one inside and one outside which helps when the club has to have segregated games.

The club currently has an U19's team and a link to a separate local youth club. They are looking to develop a youth system in the future. They also have links to the college whereby a player from the club goes there and coaches, receiving at the same time two wages. One as a player and one as a coach for the local youth team. Believe it or not, there is only one paid member of staff (besides the playing squad), and that is Lee Bullock, who is the Commercial Director who of course generates income for the club. Lee originally came as a player, then a manager. Everyone else here are volunteers including a great ambassador to the club in the form of Managing Director Graeme Hinchcliffe. Yet another club and ground well worth a visit.

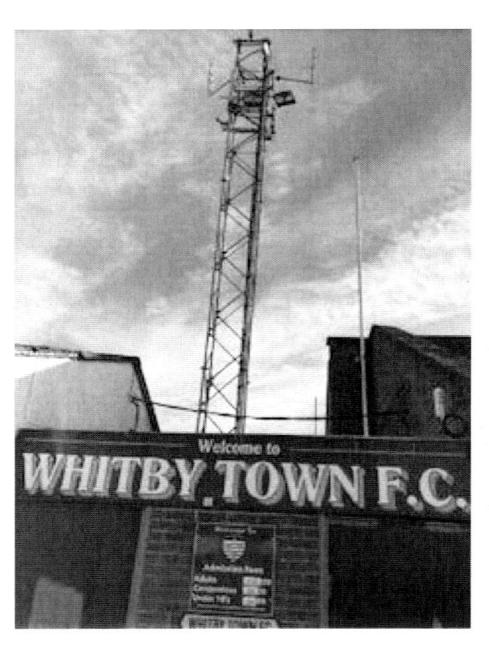

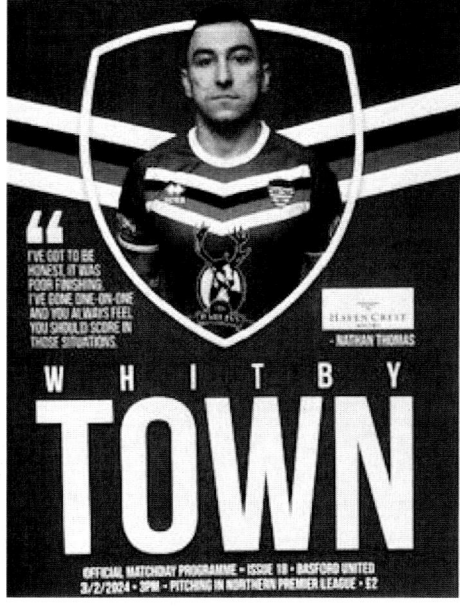

WINCHESTER CITY V MERTHYR TOWN
SOUTHERN PREMIER LEAGUE SOUTH

16/04/24

SEARCHING FOR KING ALFRED IN WINCHESTER! Yes, they dig up everywhere in the City looking for him, but we're here to see Winchester City v Merthyr Town in this Southern Premier League South fixture.

Winchester sitting comfortable in the table after getting promotion from step 4 last season, and Merthyr are in a play off position currently so all to play for. Let battle commence England v Wales in this respectable part of the world in Hampshire!

On a lovely sunny Spring evening its 1-0 to the citizens in red(home team)after 25 mins on their grass pitch - at present. Merthyr are playing in blue & black stripes, which is incidentally Winchesters away kit. Merthyr's kit man drove down from South Wales and forgot their kit! ….then on the stroke of HT it's 2-0 to Winchester with a great move down the left hand side. The second half develops into a frantic cup tie with attacking and defending galore from both sides. Winchester hold on with some great defending and right near the end Merthyr's no.5 gets a straight red and seconds later it's a full time of 2-0 to the hosts.

The ground is named the Charters Community Stadium with the clubhouse/boardroom/changing rooms to the left of the turnstiles facing the corner flag. The main stand has covered seating and is a few feet back from the tarmac and away from the pitch. The opposite side has dug outs although very antiquated and wooden, and a covered terraced stand. Also, further down, towards the far end corner flag is a scaffolding structure to shelter in. Behind the nearest goal is an identikit stand and wooden surrounds set back from the goal. The opposite goal end is just grass - for training on perhaps. To note, alongside the main stand mentioned, there was another stand which has just been dismantled.

During this close season, the current pitch will be dug up and an artificial pitch laid. The main stand will be moved nearer to the pitch. All the current perimeter fencing of wire mesh, iron poles, wooden structure, will all be replaced with new. Another new stand will be built alongside the main stand. There will also be a refurb of the clubhouse, which is looking very tired and dated now. There is so much more scope to build around this ground, and I see vast improvements over the forthcoming years.

The cost of the 3G pitch is going to be met by a grant from the Football Foundation(the club has to put in a small token amount). Although its taken 4 years to get the grant signed off and was actually signed off today! The 3G pitch usage has a trust set up for a non profit making organisation. Any surplus to go on the refurb of the clubhouse - the club have to generate funds to do this so they become self sufficient. The wi fi needs upgrading as no signal as its on the old copper wire. Having such stalwarts at the club as Secretary Jon McLaren and Chairman Ken Raisbeck have helped steer Winchester city in the right direction.

Expansion plans - Need to have 500 covered seats & 500 standing in place before next season and have special dispensation to do this, because of digging up their pitch at the end of this season and doing all the works at the same time. New LED floodlights are to be installed as well as a new car park. all this at a total cost of £1.4 M funded by the football Foundation and the local council.

The scaffolding stand was just pro temp for this season and will be dismantled. A new club shop is to be installed in a lock up container, adjoined with a new burger bar, both to be situated next to the main stand. That's handy as you wont have to go too far to buy your burger and new scarf! The club shop is currently being shared with the game announcer.

This is the clubs 4th ground overall. Previously they were at the City dump, the army pitch, and the King George 5th playing fields. Asbestos was found underneath the spare ground next to the pitch therefore causing postponements of games.

Where they are is an area of natural scientific interest with a river either side of the ground. Its medieval and made to flood where the pitch is - its protected so the club cant do anything about it! They also have to create a green path from the pitch to the river to protect the wildlife.

The future looks bright with the club and all the up and coming new surfaces and facilities, not only that but the club has 37 youth teams, plus Ladies team, disability team, so all in all a total of 65 teams.

The club were originally formed in 1884 as Winchester Swallows FC. They changed their name to Winchester FC, then in 1907 to the present name.

1971/72 joining the Southern League briefly before re joining the Hampshire League. 2001/02 - the club merged with Winchester Castle and the following season they achieved the treble of winning the league and two cups. 2004/04 - Won the FA vase beating AFC Sudbury, but ground grading denied them the chance to get promoted back to the Southern League.

WORKSOP TOWN V SHEFFIELD WEDNESDAY
PRE SEASON FRIENDLY

30/07/24

South of Sheffield, with a 3 hour journey from London, i arrive at Worksop Town for their friendly with local rivals Sheffield Wednesday!

In time for a run down on the club with Chairman Pete Whitehead. A great club with a lovely feel about the place and the meeting set up via Life President Keith Ilett. This club has certainly been transformed since Pete took over. Pete was invited by Keith back in 2018/19 as the club were in dire financial difficulties. Pete has turned this club around from a £250K debt to a club that is fully sustainable with no financial worries.

Going back to 1922 though and the FA cup 1st round(equivalent to R3 today). The club played Spurs away and they sent a team of miners to play a team of Internationals. Against all the odds the score ended 0-0. Instead of a replay back at Worksop, the directors of Spurs showed Worksop a good time around London, plied them with drink, and put them all up in a hotel. They agreed to stay over 2 nights to replay the game at Spurs again and were thrashed 9-0. After the first game, there was a band waiting at Worksop station to greet the team home. They obviously never arrived and the directors of the club were never forgiven for this! The club folded briefly in 1930.

Worksop have owned their present ground since 2012 and were previously at the Don Valley Stadium. They found Sandy Lane as Sheffield Parramore sports invited Worksop Town to come back and be landlords. In 2018/19, the club were in financial difficulty and Pete Whitehead was contacted by Keith Illet to help out financially. Pete came on board, took over the club and raised funds. During the covid period the ground was redeveloped. A new 3G pitch was laid, the stand was redeveloped including the changing rooms. They now have in place an academy, 27 junior teams overall ranging from U8 to U16 as well as a reserve team & U21's. The facilities here operate 7 days a week with 500 kids and adults.

There is a pathway from the youth to 1st team and the U16 are involved in an education programme where they go on a B tech course with a view to getting sports qualifications. The club works closely with their neighbours at Wednesday and United in Sheffield, and also with Doncaster and Rotherham. With the academy the trials are on a quarterly basis and they use the loan system very well.

The first team have broken a number of records - in season 2022/23 they went unbeaten over 37 games (going back to 1977 when Boston held the record). This is non league on a whole this record. They also won the league by February of that season scoring over 100 goals. Their leading goal scorer, with 49 goals, was Liam Hughes who was also the player of the year over steps 3 & 4. Other players of note are Sam Wedgebury, Jay Rollings (ex Boston), and Paul Green an Ireland International with 25 caps.

Within the local community, the club work with local schools coaching kids, via their academy. Their current charity, they sponsor a different one each year, is 'Aurora'. They deal with mental health after one of their players sadly committed suicide shortly after emigrating.

The 3G pitch was built in 2020 and is maintained weekly. It is renowned as a FIFA quality programme pitch and the fibres are triple stitched, as opposed to single, and tested annually. All of this has been self financed by the owner, therefore no restrictions from the Football Foundation.

Another proud fact is the club also hold the record jointly, along with Sheffield Wednesday and Frickley, for the joint highest wins - 14 - of the Sheffield & Hallamshire Senior Trophy. The ribbons on the trophy are Worksop colours as the current holders. This is the 3rd oldest active cup still played for in Britain after the FA cup & Scottish cup.

Tonight's game there is a crowd of over 800 and Worksop go 1-0 up, after 16 mins, through Vaughan Redford. The same player grabs his second on 32 mins. On 59 mins it's 3-0 with a great cross to Jordan Burrow, and 3 mins later it's now 4-0 from Dan Brammell. There's been some great assured goalkeeping from the No.1 Tommy Taylor (ex Darlington) and it seems the home team in grey & black are going to do far better than the away team in blue & white stripes this season!

Had a great birds eye view of the game tonight from the boardroom balcony and the ground is impressive and being continually updated with new turnstiles which are just about to operate. Incidentally the clubs biggest ever crowd was against a local side in a real Worksop derby v St Joseph's, when over 2,000 turned up for a cup game!

YATELEY UNITED V MOLESEY

COMBINED COUNTIES CHALLENGE CUP SEMI FINAL

14/05/24

Just when you thought you've been to the last game of the season, up pops this semi final of the Esoteric Combined Counties Division cup semi final. Two teams from the top half of their division(step 6) Yateley United FC v Moseley FC. A crowd of 139 cries out for every little tackle and foul. The players are all looking fit, but it's the ref who looks as though he's eaten all the pies!

Yateley United, a club that formed as recently as 2013, came together from 4 clubs - Yateley Town, Yateley Juniors, Yateley Green, and Beaulieu boys & girls FC. The President - Colin Ive - and drive behind the club, states there was a Yateley FC going back to 1923. In 1985 there was a split and the clubs formed from that split were Yateley Green & Yateley Town. The club - Yateley Town - got together in 2010 to formulate a plan to raise funds to keep the club going and to go forward.They only needed a cool £1 million, and yes they came up with the idea of let's do a music festival! It worked and going back to 2011 was their first music festival, and they've now been going for 14 years successfully. This is their main fund raiser but they also have a beer & wine festival to double up with funds!

Colin described themselves as a commodity club and a business. There was originally a club called Yateley FC going back to 1923, but we're looking at the more recent history, and in 2014 they contacted a local cement mixing company - Cemex - to sell land advertised at £70K. It was bought for £60K and they now own the land on a short lease. They concentrated firstly on digging up the pitch, whereby they spent a further £70K on a new pitch and drainage. 50% of this came form the Football Foundation in 2016, then on to building the clubhouse. The rest of the money was raised from the festivals.

In 2018 they received planning permission for the floodlights to be erected, on which the pitch is now used 7 days a week. To raise funds they had meals with football celebrities including the likes of Peter Shilton & Mark Wright attending.

In October 2022, the clubhouse was officially opened by Ossie Ardiles(his grandsons play for Yateley Youth), and is now used regularly and hired out for functions. Their first inaugural game under the flood lights was in September 2023 with a crowd of 400 - their current average crowd is 150.

In 2023, they won the Thames Valley Premier League(step 7)and were promoted into the main pyramid system up to step 6.They have finished their first season in step 6 in a very creditable 7th position.

The budget for each year is raised from the music festival and an existing loan and they have plans, and ambitions, to go further up the ladder to step 4 and 3.

None of the players are paid and the only volunteers paid are the bar staff. A very loyal local set of people. A Community club has also been created from the family festivals. They have a total of 32 youth teams plus 8 adult teams, including the ladies team who have just won their league. Incidentally one of their ladies plays in the deaf world cup! The teams range from U6 to age 85 where they have walk in football, and one of those players is a disabled international.

They have continued to keep the name of Devereux Park, which was named after a local missionary for the Catholic church in Africa. The Community Centre Ltd run the bar and Yateley Sports Community and the International company runs the festivals. This is more advantageous for tax reasons I've been informed. As for the land, the club own it now entirely.

The team is run by Sam Wilson, a local volunteer of a team of 8 who run the playing side. Its run on the same basis as a top Premier club. As for the future, they are going to build a 3g pitch to make the pitch into an all round usable asset. They are currently talking with a number of organisations to this end.

To describe the ground - the large clubhouse is facing onto the pitch set onto a large patio area. There is a small seated covered stand on that side. Opposite there are just dug outs(which backs onto the youth pitches). Behind one goal is a small covered stand and the opposite end is just a walkway

The match…1-0 to Yateley on the stroke of HT. Back into the clubhouse to what I must say is the best bite I've had at football. You must try the veggie chicken gujons in a bun. Pure munch! Out for the second half, 10 mins gone and it's all square now at 1-1. Then right near the end it's Molesey that get their second and looks like the winner. In the last min.one of the home players is laying down on the pitch, for at least 10 mins with a head injury. When he's finally strapped up, thank goodness, and helped off the pitch, Yateley nearly get an equaliser in the dying seconds. To no avail it's Molesey v Westside in the cup final to played at Sheerwater FC.

BISHOP AUCKLAND MUSEUM

30/03/24

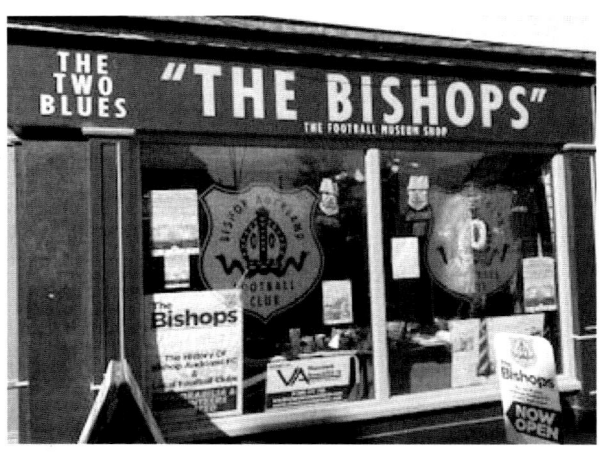

An Easter weekend trip to County Durham and taking in this Museum/shop in Bishop Auckland. It's the only one of it's kind in the country. A museum dedicated to mostly one club outside, and away, from the football ground. A real history of the most famous Amateur club in this country, who actually won 10 of the 18 FA Amateur cup finals they appeared in. Easily a record and an outstanding one at that. Can you imagine now two non league teams like Bishop Auckland & Hendon playing in a cup final at Wembley with a crowd of over 100,000. Well it did happen back in the mid 50's.

The club also has an affiliation with Man Utd, going back to the plane disaster of 1958 when they helped United out by giving them 3 of their best players to survive and continue playing games, when at that time Man Utd could have discontinued their season due to a lack of players - due to deaths and injuries. They also had no less than Bob Paisley (Liverpool's past manager with the most trophies won!)playing for the great Auckland side. The chaps inside the museum will give you a great historical insight into the club, and when you hear them tell it, you feel you are actually re living it yourself. Not only that but Barry Tray will also educate you with true stories of what it was like working down the coal pits of County Durham. That's another story in itself and those miners were so courageous and heroes to this country. You can't imagine anybody wanting to work down the pits nowadays no matter how much money they were offered, and it wasn't much in those days.

This is a must see museum in the centre of Bishop Auckland. You'll also 'bump' into the club chairman who goes in most days. With its array of trophies, programmes, original shirts, team photos, as well as recent books for sale and current club merchandise. Most of the memorabilia has come from Geoff & Barbara Wood - from the Durham Amateur Football Trust - and well put together here. If you're into football and history then you won't be disappointed, and why not tie it in with a Bishop Auckland, or Crook Town, or West Auckland home game - 3 cracking clubs to say the least!

You will also see memorabilia and history on other County Durham clubs like West Auckland(first World cup winners), and Crook Town - a force to be reckoned with alongside the Bishops back in the day.

WOOLWICH WANDERERS V NEWTON HEATH
FRIENDLY

03/09/1923

The Sunday game and it's the top two non league sides - Woolwich Wanderers v Newton Heath. SE London v up north. Despite the nice weather the game has been rescheduled to a new park in North London. There is a rumour that Woolwich Wanderers will change their name to the Arse and play north of the river….it'll never catch on!

They have managed to acquire a new player from Thames Ironworks, an Irishman by the name of Dec O'Rice whom they played a billion trillion roubles for. Newton Heath, not to be outdone have signed Johnny Le Foreigner from Athletico Useless for a new football(with tie ups and a pigs bladder inside)and a pack of porn paying cards.

The Wanderers line up with a new attacking formation of 1-3-6 with the intention of booting it upfield and hope someone kicks it past the goalie Johnny Fatpud. Newton Heath don't have a formation as such but were overheard saying "We'll just kick these Southern softies off the pitch"….so, the same tactics as the last game then!

First blood comes to the Heath as Marc the rash man takes on the square defence and leaves them flat footed with a great strike. Within a minute the Wanderers equalise with a carefully placed goal from Johnny de Gaard which leaves the fat keeper flat footed.

The players trot off for their half time oranges, and a sneaky fag, whilst the Manager, Johnny da Teta, talks bollox whilst combing his hair in the mirror. Hmmm.

Into the second half and the home crowd of 12,000 packed into the roped off park in Highbury Fields, are questioning where the **** the ref has come from 'cos he's shite!

Near the end the Heath score a great goal which looks like the winner, and then the ref changes his mind after his mates from the secret society - Voice against reason(or VAR for short)say no, bungs the ref a three Penny bit(in a brown envelope)so no goal!

The game is nearly over till the ref shouts out "next goal wins"!...and then it's down to the Irishman O'Rice to slice a wild kick, hits two players, and bounces into the goal past Fatpud(who has clearly eaten all the pies at half time). Rather than blow the whistle, the ref decides to play a few more minutes, just for the hell of it….until the Wanderers send a ball through to their part time footballer, and local priest, Johnny Jesus. He slides the ball between the two wooden posts and HURRAH! It's 3-1 to the Wanderers.

This modern football lark will never catch on.

ASCOT UNITED F.C.
Welcome to ...
Ascot United
www.ascotunited.net

Blyth Spartans AFC
SPARTANS SOUL
KEEP THE FAITH
Amble Branch

COME ON BOYS
NORTH GREENFORD UTD
STRONGER TOGETHER

BATH

CHESHAM UNITED

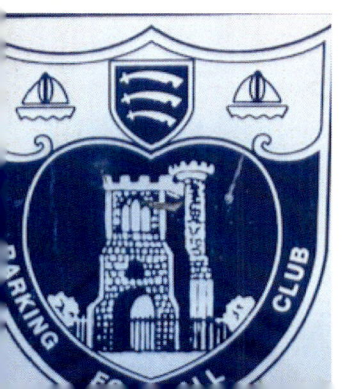

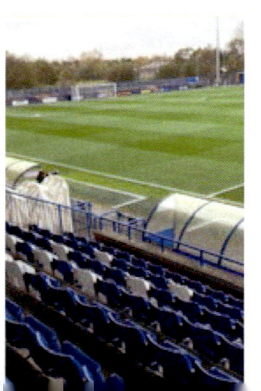

Welcome to SOUTHEND UNITED FOOTBALL CLUB

HARBOROUGH TOWN FC
Craig Robinson   Memorial Stand

Yarmouth and District Archaeological
This Grandstand
was officially opened on
11th June 1892
and is thought to be the oldest
surviving Football Grandstand
in England

ACKNOWLEDGEMENTS

Martin Isaacs, Andy Sawyer, Paul Fenner, Tim Mardell (Bath City),
Trevor Knell, Chris Hewitt (the mighty North Greenford United!),
Steve Crump, Col Robson, Ruth Hetherington (Darlington),
Keith Vernon, Jason Laybourne (Warrington Loyal), Toby Kinder,
Rob Hoult, Derek Crow-Bell (Ramsgate), Barry Tray (Bishop Museum),
Kevin Mayes, James Collins (Bower & Pitsea), Alan Whittaker,
Tom McKie (Alnwick Town), Paul Hallam, Martin Baxter (Great Yarmouth),
Jenny Blackhall (Berwick), Alice Dewey (Cambridge City),
Laurence Jones (Harborough Town), Bob Knightly (Romford),
James Lawson (Ramsgate), Darrell Osborne (Tring Athletic),
Scott Booth (Whitby Town).